ON GOLF

ON GOLF

LESSONS FROM AMERICA'S MASTER TEACHER

○○○

JIM FLICK

WITH GLEN WAGGONER

VILLARD

NEW YORK

Published in the United States by Villard Books, a division of Random House, Inc., New York, and simultaneously in Canada by Random House of Canada, Limited, Toronto.

Originally published in hardcover by Villard Books, a division of Random House, Inc., in 1997.

VILLARD BOOKS is a registered trademark of Random House, Inc.
Colophon is a trademark of Random House, Inc.

Library of Congress Cataloging-in-Publication Data

Flick, Jim.
On golf: lessons from America's master teacher / by Jim Flick with Glen Waggoner.
p. cm.
ISBN 0-375-75706-6
1. Golf—Study and teaching. 2. Golf—Psychological aspects.
I. Waggoner, Glen. II. Title.
GV962.5.F55 1997
796.352'07—dc21 96-29587

Villard website address: www.villard.com
Printed in the United States of America on acid-free paper
24689753
First Paperback Edition

To the many, many golfers I have known and worked with over the years, from top professionals to rank beginners, who have taught me everything I know about the greatest game of them all . . .

To the memory of my father, Coleman Denny Flick, the best golf partner I have ever had. He gave me his love for the game and its challenges, along with so much more . . .

And finally, to my wonderfully talented wife, Geri, whose creativity and imagination are a constant source of inspiration.

FOREWORD

by Jack Nicklaus

A GREAT TEACHER IN golf is that rare individual who's able to go beyond the mechanics of the golf swing and take a genuine personal interest in the individual he's teaching. If Jack Grout hadn't taken a personal interest in an eager ten-year-old kid back in Columbus, Ohio—an interest in him as a person that went beyond teaching him how to play a game—I might never have become a golfer. It was that commitment to helping a person discover what he is capable of doing, not just teaching some formula, that set Jack Grout apart.

Jim Flick is that kind of teacher.

I first met Jim back in 1961 in Cincinnati, where he was the head pro at the Losantiville Golf Club. While I found him extremely personable and engaging, our paths didn't cross that much at first. Later, in the 1970s and 1980s, I began to see more of Jim at Frenchman's Creek in North Palm Beach, where I worked regularly with Mr. Grout. Jim, who by then was a widely respected golf teacher in his own right, would come by and quietly observe us. By nature Jim is a thoughtful, inquisitive person, and I think one of his great strengths is his power of observation.

But it wasn't until 1990, at the PGA Senior Tour's Tradition golf tournament at Desert Mountain in Scottsdale, Arizona, that I became fully aware of what a keen observer and gifted teacher Jim Flick really is.

The Tradition was my first tournament on the Senior Tour. On Tuesday afternoon, as I was heading out to play the golf course, I ran into Jim, who asked if he could come along with me. I hadn't worked with anyone since we lost Mr. Grout the previous year, so I was happy to have an opportunity to get Jim's input. As we walked up the eighteenth fairway, I asked Jim what he saw in my swing. He looked me in the eye and said, "What I don't see is Jack Nicklaus."

We headed right to the practice range, and that was when I started working with Jim Flick. I went on to win the golf tournament, and I have been working with Jim ever since.

After Jim and I had been working together about a year, Jim approached me with an idea for making sure that the principles and the approach to the game that I had first learned from Mr. Grout—and that Jim had developed over four decades of teaching—were passed on to future students of the game. That idea became the foundation of the Nicklaus-Flick Golf School, which we established in 1991.

As much as anyone I've ever known, Jim understands that people have different abilities, different rhythms, and different timing, so one swing isn't going to be right for everybody. He begins with a simple goal: to help a golfer feel where his club head is and then use it to find the ball. He teaches you to swing the golf club—and not to get tied up by golf mechanics.

Most important, though, is that Jim helps people understand and love the game of golf. His enthusiasm and commitment are infectious. When I talk to people who are repeat students at the Nicklaus-Flick Golf School, I get the feeling that they come back more just to spend time with Jim Flick than to improve their games.

The purpose of playing golf, after all, is to have fun and to enjoy yourself. I've never met anyone better at helping people enjoy themselves and have fun on the golf course than Jim. That's because he brings to his teaching the commitment I mentioned earlier, the hallmark of a great teacher.

That personal commitment is the driving force behind this book and the legacy of a great golf teacher, Jim Flick.

CONTENTS

INTRODUCTION

by Tom Lehman

THE YEAR WAS 1990, and I was in desperate need of help. I was playing on the Hogan Tour—it's now called the Nike Tour—and really struggling with my wedge game. From a hundred yards on in I was just pitiful. The courses we played were mostly driver-wedge, and if I couldn't get my wedges on the green, I was going to be in trouble. Big trouble.

I knew Jim Flick was one of the best teachers in the world, and we had just moved to Scottsdale, so I called him at Desert Mountain, where he's based when he's not off at one of his Nicklaus-Flick Golf Schools. I told him I needed some help in that one particular area of my game.

Well, he said he was very busy and wasn't sure he had the time, but I kind of begged him. Just a little bit. Well, okay, a lot. Finally, I said I just wanted to come out and watch him give someone else a lesson.

He said he'd call me back, and he hung up. I found out later that he'd called up a couple of the players on the tour who lived in the area and asked, "What kind of person is this Lehman fellow? Is he serious about getting better?"

They said, yes, he's a good player, even though he can barely make a cut—you should see him. And so Jim called me back, told me to come see him at noon the next day, and that was the beginning.

After talking with Jim about his philosophy in that very first session, I realized his approach in helping with my little wedges could also work with my chipping. And my driving. In fact, it could work with all parts of my game. And that's exactly what happened.

We've worked together over six years now, and we haven't gotten off our game plan. Other teachers I'd been to, they'd start here, then go off on one tangent, then onto another, and pretty soon I'd be so wrapped up with thoughts that I couldn't even play. With Jim, our focus hasn't wavered. It is totally consistent.

Jim is almost like a sports psychologist. His belief in my game, and his belief in me as a person, come through in his teaching. Whenever I go to him to get a lesson, I always leave feeling uplifted, both professionally and personally. I've seen the same thing happen with amateurs he works with. That's what I think makes him so appealing to everybody—people leave his lessons feeling good about the game of golf and about life in general.

Jim realizes that there's no such thing as having the perfect golf swing. You need to take what you have and make it as good as you can get it. To get to that point, Jim works on your attitude, your perseverance, your heart, your patience. All the little intangibles. It's those intangibles that either take a guy to the top or leave him where he is. Very few people stay where they are after Jim Flick gets through with them.

Jim understands the overall golf swing better than anyone I've ever met. He can also communicate that understanding, whether he's working with a pro or an average golfer. He relays information to you so you can understand it. You know, you could have ten guys tell you the same thing, but unless you understand it and feel it, you really can't improve.

One of my closest friends started working with Jim a few years after I did. My friend was a good golfer who'd hit a plateau—he wasn't getting any better, no matter how much he played and practiced. Jim took him back to basics, to fundamentals, and over a four-year period, my friend lowered his handicap eight strokes, from a six to a plus two.

Back when I first started working with Jim, the idea of winning a major championship was totally outside the realm of possibility. It was not even something I considered. To have come this far is just thrilling. When I won the 1996 British Open, it sent tingles down my back, chills down my spine. I would not have had those chills if it weren't for Jim Flick.

It's a long process. In this book, Jim gives you the right stuff to work on and inspires you to work on it. Now, if you *want* to work on it, you *will* improve. But you just have to take it step by step and have patience. This isn't a game where there are any secrets or any shortcuts.

Perhaps the most appealing thing about Jim's teaching technique is that he never, ever loses sight of the fact that it's all about *playing* golf, not *working* it. He teaches you how to get the ball in the hole as quickly as possible, which is, after all, what golf is all about. But, in the process, he makes it fun and interesting. He makes you *want* to get better, and he makes you *want* to do it the right way. The thing that I appreciate most about Jim's approach, I guess, is that the things we worked on in the very first lesson are the things we're *still* working on.

The only thing that's changed is that I'm getting better. And if you listen to Jim Flick, you'll get better, too.

ON GOLF

LESSON 1

A TEACHER'S EDUCATION

I GREW UP IN the huge, thriving metropolis of Bedford, Indiana, smack-dab in the middle of Middle America before anybody ever called it that. We knew a little about basketball in Bedford, not much about golf, and a whole lot about doing what we were told by our elders.

So when somebody told me that the key to the golf swing was keeping the left elbow straight, well, I straightened that sucker out and didn't bend it for about ten years. Then somebody else told me to keep my head down and—plunk!—my chin hit my chest and stayed there. Turn my shoulders to start the backswing? You got it. Drive my hips? Accelerate through impact? Finish high? I'm your man.

Pretty soon I was a fine-tuned, high-octane golfing machine. And that was my problem. If there's one thing I've learned in nearly five decades of teaching, playing, and loving golf, it's that golf is *not* a game of mechanics. It's a game of *feel*.

The high-octane part? That refers to the attitude I took out on the golf course. If I hit a less-than-perfect shot, I'd give myself a serious going-over. And if I hit a *bad* shot? Well, high-octane fuel burns really fast. You can't have a self-punishing attitude and play golf up to your natural abilities. You have to be your own best friend out on the golf course. It took me a long time to learn that.

I loved all sports. Still do. I played basketball (in Indiana, when I was growing up, there was a local law that said you had to). I did a little competitive diving. I played a little baseball. I followed football (with my scrawny build, that was as close as I could afford to get). But golf was just something I did to fill up my summers. At first.

My father introduced me to golf, and the most fun I've ever had in the game was playing with him. Dad was a scratch player. He caddied for Walter Hagen when he won the 1924 PGA Championship held in French Lick, Indiana, a place now best known as the hometown of Larry Bird but back then famous for its popular resort and two Donald Ross golf courses. My father really knew and loved golf, and he instinctively understood how to communicate that knowledge and love to me.

What does having fun in golf mean? Different things to different people, but to me, it starts with recognizing, accepting, and enjoying the challenges offered by the game. Simple as golf is—you knock a little white ball around a field, then tap it into a hole in the ground; how much simpler can you get?—it is also a game of infinite subtlety and possibility. And the door that leads to its inner secrets and rewards is marked *fun*.

By the time I went off to Wake Forest on a basketball scholarship, though, I was good enough to play on the Deacons' golf team. If you follow golf at all, you know that Wake Forest has sent some mighty fine players onto the PGA Tour: Curtis Strange . . . Lanny Wadkins . . . Jay Haas . . . Scott Hoch . . . Jay Siegel. I wasn't one of them, but my roommate for a while was a pretty good Wake Forest golfer. A kid from Pennsylvania named Arnold Palmer.

Even back then, Arnold had this enormous competitive spirit, this fire and passion for the game. He could *will* the ball into the target area, stare the damned thing into the hole. He attacked the golf course. And later, after a round, he could laugh hardest at the times the golf course fought back.

One time, when Arnold and I were playing on a little nine-hole course on the Wake Forest campus, we both drove our balls into the right rough on the third hole. His ball was thirty yards in front of mine, of course, but both of us faced tough second shots.

Well, as I was walking up the fairway, head down and chewing my sorry butt out for making a bad swing, I looked up and there was Arnold, way up ahead of me in the rough. He had found his ball, checked his lie, figured out just how he was going to bend it around some trees, taken a practice swing, and knocked his ball onto the green—while I was trudging up the fairway, stewing in my own juices.

Arnold hadn't wasted an ounce of effort dwelling on what went wrong with his first swing. While I was trying to evaluate the reason for my bad shot, he was looking for the best way to get his ball back in play. While I was thinking about my *last* shot, he was thinking about his *next* shot.

I was too dumb at the time to realize what I was seeing and experiencing, but what it came down to was this: I was *working* golf, and Arnold was *playing* golf.

❍

After graduating from Wake Forest with a business degree, I was drafted into the army and served two years at the time of the Korean War. By then, golf had sort of taken over my dreams, so I turned professional, apprenticed at a couple of clubs in Indiana, and was named, in 1961, head pro at the Losantiville Golf Club in Cincinnati.

(By the way, Losantiville was the second name of the Ohio River town that later became Cincinnati. The original, early-nineteenth-century settlement was called Porkopolis, I suppose because the early settlers were expert hog breeders and traders. In a way, it's too bad the name didn't stick. Instead of pulling for the Cincinnati Bengals, as I still do, I could be rooting for the Porkopolis Pigs.)

Losantiville was—and is—one of the best golf clubs in the Midwest, with a membership that takes its golf very seriously indeed. It was at Losantiville that I first met the Ohio State golfer everybody in that part of the country was buzzing about: Jack Nicklaus.

The year before, Jack had won the U.S. Pro-Am—a scratch event, with no handicaps—as an amateur. This year, the tournament was held again at Losantiville, and he won as a professional. You didn't have to be a golf genius to realize all that buzzing was well founded.

During the sixties, I taught at Losantiville, conducted PGA clinics, and worked with a handful of leading pros, among them Susie Maxwell Berning, who won three U.S. Open titles; Hollis Stacy, who won eighteen LPGA Tour events; and the late Burt Yancey on the PGA Tour. All this time I kept up with Jack Nicklaus's career—who didn't?—but had only casual contact with him.

In 1972, my life and teaching career took a critical turn when Bob Toski invited me out to Silverado, the northern California golf resort, to watch him conduct one of the schools he had recently set up for *Golf Digest*. There Bob opened my eyes to what golf teaching is all about. I could tell he was a genius at getting people to respond in a more instinctive way to playing the game. I could also tell how much I had to learn about teaching the game. When Bob invited me to work with him in the *Golf Digest* schools, I jumped at the chance. I worked with him a few schools a year at first, then a dozen, until finally, in 1976, I left Losantivlle to become a full-time faculty member under "Dean" Toski.

Bob and I shared a lot of ideas, and when we differed, we always found ways to blend them. For instance, I have always put a lot of emphasis on a good setup, while Bob prefers to focus on free swinging with the arms. I came to understand that you needed both. I think we complemented each other very well. To this day, I still feel that most of the concepts I teach have evolved from things that Bob Toski taught me.

We had a lot of success and even more fun with the *Golf Digest* schools, and by the mid-eighties, with the huge boom in golf's popularity, new golf schools, teaching facilities, and clinics were popping up all over the country. A lot of these operations emphasized high-tech teaching aids, computer simulations of the "perfect" golf swing, and—to our profession's discredit, in my opinion—an approach that focused on the *mechanics of the golf swing* rather than on *playing golf.*

❍

From time to time over the years, mostly at Frenchman's Creek Golf Club in North Palm Beach, I would watch Jack Nicklaus work with his longtime teacher, Jack Grout. But we never had an extended talk about golf until 1990 at the Tradition, the first Senior Tour event that Jack ever played in. He'd been having trouble with his game, knew I'd seen him work with Mr. Grout, who'd recently passed away, and asked me what I saw in his swing.

I told him I did *not* see Jack Nicklaus in that golf swing. He asked me what I meant, and I told him, "Jack, you don't *feel* your club head anymore." I could tell that because the speed of his body was out of kilter with the old Nicklaus golf swing. I reminded him that one of Mr. Grout's cardinal rules was that he must change direction from backswing to forward swing from the ground up with his feet and knees. I saw him initiating the change of direction with his body and hips, and it was interfering with his swing. He was trying to work his body so hard that he had lost feel for the golf club.

I must have struck a responsive chord because we started working together that very day, and I've been coaching Jack ever since. I say "coaching" rather than "teaching" because I wouldn't presume to teach anything to the greatest golfer ever to play the game. I didn't try then to give him anything new, nor have I since. I have just helped him keep in touch with the basic principles his game is built on, the principles that form the bedrock of the Nicklaus-Flick Golf School, which Jack and I founded in 1991.

❍

Over the years, I have worked with U.S. Open champions and thirty handicappers, professionals struggling to keep their tour cards and amateurs struggling to get into the eighties, men, women, and—the most fun of all—kids.

I have been privileged to work with Jack Nicklaus, whose unsurpassed understanding and feel for the game of golf are, I hope, reflected in this book.

Recently I've been working with Tom Lehman, a young man who lost his tour card three times but who in 1996 won the British Open, won the PGA Tour Championship, won the Vardon Trophy, won more money than anybody on the PGA Tour, and won Player of the Year honors. But Tom is a winner, as far as I'm concerned, not because of all that but because of the courage, determination, and integrity he brings to his game and his life.

What kind of book is this going to be? *Not* a traditional, comprehensive, soup-to-nuts how-to book. I don't think that's what the average golfer needs. The problem isn't that there's not enough information available about how to play golf; it's that there may be too much.

Moreover, it isn't the way I teach. A fellow comes to me looking for help, I don't sit him down and tell him everything I've ever learned, heard, or suspected about golf. The first thing I do is listen. I try to get inside his mind, find out what kind of temperament he has, what level of commitment to improvement his lifestyle permits, how he feels about himself and his abilities. I'm certainly no shrink, but I can't begin to fix a guy's golf swing until I've fixed his mind.

By "fix" I mean equip him with a concept that will help him play the game. Without a basic concept to guide him, the average golfer becomes a sitting duck for the barrage of tips, nostrums, and panaceas fired at him these days from books, magazines, tapes, golf instructors, TV, his own playing partners, equipment ads, the Internet, and, for all I know, outer space. I want to try to simplify things a little bit, give you a basic concept, a few concrete principles, and some guidelines for building your own game and becoming your own coach.

My main reason for writing this book is that, in my opinion, there are three big problems with the way the game of golf has been taught in recent years:

1. Too much emphasis has been placed on turning the shoulders and hips first in the golf swing—that is, on *making a conscious effort* to shift one's weight instead of letting a weight shift occur naturally in response to the swinging of the golf club. Too much emphasis on turning the shoulders and hips, too little on swinging the golf club.
2. Too much emphasis in instruction today is based on what the tour pros do. I believe we can all learn a lot from the great golfers. Goodness knows, I have. But most golfers

lack the ability, the experience, the physical makeup, and the training to play golf the way the pros do. It may seem like the same game, but it isn't.

3. Too much emphasis has been put on the mechanics of the golf swing. Golf is a game of feel: you'll read these words dozens of times in the following pages because I can't stress it enough. Consciously focusing on swing mechanics *while on the golf course* robs a player of his ability to feel and play golf.

Who is this book for?

Not primarily for the scratch player, although what I have to say concerning the mental and emotional aspects of the game will, I believe, be useful to golfers at all levels.

This book is primarily for the golfer who's played enough to know how demanding, exasperating, and wonderful the game can be—all in the space of a single hole.

My personal goal is to help people play better, not turn them into swing freaks. I believe the best approach to golf is based not on mechanical manipulation of the golf instrument but on a *feel* for playing the game.

To that effect, I emphasize a nonmechanical, *feel* approach to golf in this book. I describe a pendulum-like swing that's better suited, in my opinion, to most golfers than the "one-piece takeaway" and "big-muscle" theories so widely taught today. I explain the critical importance of grip, posture, and the body's swinging elements. I tell you how to practice smart—and how to work on your game when you can't go to the course. And I talk a lot—a *lot*—about the attitude you need to play golf, the commitment, the patience, the willingness to work hard to get better.

What works best in life also works best in golf. You need honesty, creativity, and a positive but realistic attitude to play

Please Accept My Apology

The National Golf Foundation calculates that of the 25 million Americans who played at least one round of golf last year, fully 21.5 percent—or 5,375,000—are women. Furthermore, of the 19,625,000 men who played at least one round, 4.3 percent—or 843,875—are left-handed.

That means in the following pages I have deliberately, but entirely without malice, risked offending 6,218,875 women and left-handed golfers—and that's not even counting the 231,125 left-handed women golfers whom I may have offended twice.

I'm referring, of course, to the he-she and right-left conundrum. Had I written "he or she" and "him or her" every time those pronouns were called for, *and* duplicated instructions on where to place your "left/right" hands on the club, this book would weigh more than a tour pro's golf bag.

I teach a lot of women golfers. I teach a lot of left-handed golfers. I even teach a few left-handed women golfers. To them especially, and to others like them who are all too accustomed to slights of this nature, I do, sincerely, apologize.

golf. You need to be able to learn from failure. You need to have an inquisitive nature, sensitivity, and the ability to look at yourself clearly. You need good judgment. You also need a sense of humor. *Especially* a sense of humor.

There is no lucky-sperm club in golf. Nobody can inherit a game. Nobody can marry a game. Nobody can buy a game. If you're going to get good at golf, you have to develop the habits that let you play in situations in which you are the least comfortable. Because the golf course will find your weaknesses, the Golf Gods will put you to the test. And if you can't handle that, then get a tennis racket, put a klutz on the other side of the net, and by the klutz's standards you'll look like a star.

But golf tells it exactly like it is. You don't learn golf on your terms. You learn golf on its terms.

That's what I love and respect most about the game.

LESSON 2

LET'S *PLAY* GOLF, NOT *WORK* IT

A GAME IS SOMETHING you play to amuse yourself and have fun. The Scottish shepherds around St. Andrews who supposedly invented golf weren't looking for part-time jobs—they were looking for something to relieve their boredom. Something to *play*.

So how come so many golfers today look as if they're *working* golf instead of *playing* it?

One reason may be that golf is one of the few games—maybe the only game—in which you learn and train in a totally different environment from where you play. The practice range is vast, open, unconfining. If you hit a sideways shot, you simply pull a new ball off the pile and take another swipe. There are no hazards or penalty strokes—and there's no scorecard.

But when you go out and play, it's a far different setting. Trees and water and sand and out-of-bounds stakes threaten on all sides, and every stroke counts. It is, quite literally, a whole new ball game. Everything on the golf range is set up for success. On the golf course, everything is set up to test you.

I think the main reason people tend to work golf instead of play it is that they bring a mechanical approach—totally appropriate to the learning ground—to the golf course, the playing ground. Their bodies become prisoners of their minds. Rather than depend on the good habits they acquired through honest labor on the range and give themselves over to the nonmental, athletic activity of swinging the golf club, they repeat a mechanical, step-by-step, mistake-free-at-all-costs, mind-controlled approach that's ill suited for the playing ground.

Where did they get the mechanical approach in the first place? From golf teachers. From books. From golf magazines. From the general approach that has dominated the game at least since Ben Hogan's *Five Lessons: The Modern Fundamentals of Golf*, first published in 1957 and still in print.

It's logical: if you learn golf mechanically, it follows that you are going to play golf mechanically—or try to.

People come to a 435-yard par four with deep rough on the left and water on the right and they decide to try harder and think more about what they're doing, hoping their swing will miraculously come around. But trust me on this one because this is the key to improving your game: the more you try to impose conscious, mental control over a physical, athletic endeavor, the more tension you introduce into the equation, and the more tension you impose, the worse you will perform. You might hit some good shots, but you will not achieve consistency.

You can almost hear some people's minds clicking when they get over the ball and bring the club back. They read something somewhere, so they try to do it. Never mind that the tip they're trying to incorporate is contrary to everything else in their swing. It's a "swing thought" or a new position that they believe will put everything right. They're wrong.

The golf course is not the place to try to correct your swing. You fix things on the Training Ground. You develop habits on the Training Ground. The real challenge is implementing those habits on the Playing Ground.

Any athletic endeavor—and the golf swing is most definitely an athletic endeavor—is best done through feel and mental pictures. You want a precise identification of what your body experiences, and you want a vivid mental image of what you're trying to do. But you do not want to put all this into words and instruct your muscles to obey. They won't. They can't, not consistently.

What I want to do in these pages is sell you on an approach to learning golf based on *feel,* not mechanics. I want to help you understand how to move from the training ground to the playing ground with a mind-set—and with some basic techniques—that will let you *play* golf, not *work* it.

After all, it is a game.

> **"The psychological foundation for the most ideal state of athletic performance is that of unquestioned faith at the moment of execution."**
>
> **—Dr. Maynard Howe**

SIGN RIGHT HERE

Grab a pencil and I'll show you a little drill I sometimes use at the beginning of a Nicklaus-Flick Golf School session.

Got one? Okay, now write your name the usual way, just like you were signing a check.

Now, right under it, make as nearly an exact copy of your first signature as you can. Do it very slowly. Try to come as close to the first version as you possibly can. Take as much time as you need.

Next, take the pencil in your other hand and write your name. Try to come as close as you can to the two signatures you just did. (Don't worry, though. You won't be graded.)

Finally, with the pencil still in your "wrong" hand, write your name as rapidly as you would with your "right" hand.

What you have just done, in case you might have begun to wonder if I've gone completely off my rocker, is demonstrate the Four Levels of Learning in Golf.

Level Four, where you signed your name with your wrong hand and the outcome was just awful, we'll call *Nonconscious Incompetence.* No need to elaborate.

Level Three, where you put some time and thought into it but where the result was still pretty pathetic, represents *Conscious Incompetence.* Your conscious mind is fully in charge here, but your physical skills are woeful.

Level Two, the painstaking copy of your normal signature, is a big leap forward. Call it *Conscious Competence* because your mind is running the show *and* your physical skills are evident.

Level One, the most natural of the four signatures and the one you did with the least conscious thought, illustrates *Nonconscious Competence.*

See where I'm going with this? No? Then take a look at the differences between Levels One and Two.

My guess is that your Level Two signature looks pretty good but also a little rigid. Lines a little darker? That's because you pressed a little heavier, which means your grip pressure was a little tighter. Level One is smoother, more flowing, more natural.

Now you know where I'm going.

My guess is that most people reading this book are somewhere at Level Two or Three in their golf games. Probably some who are just starting out are at Level Four.

My goal, and I hope it's yours, is to get you to Level One.

THINK LESS, PLAY MORE

You read all the time about how much of golf is in the mind. That suggests that the more you think about your golf swing, and the harder you concentrate, the better you're going to play.

Wrong.

Dead wrong.

The golf swing takes less than a second and a half from start to finish. If your conscious mind attempts to control your swing with all sorts of mental commands—turn this, shift that—the only consistent result will be the buildup of excess tension. How could it be otherwise? There's simply no time for the body to process and respond to a bunch of conscious commands.

That's why good players prepare their conscious minds for giving up control to their subconscious with task-relevant cues. By that I mean "triggers" that activate a sequence of movements that have, through repetition, become virtually second nature.

Once you've made the decision to brush your teeth, how much is your conscious mind actively involved in the actual brushing? You learned how to brush your teeth a long time ago. You've been practicing brushing your teeth every day since then. You no longer have to think about how to brush your teeth. You just do it. Your conscious mind delegates responsibility to your subconscious.

But the subconscious can only control *learned* skills. If you haven't acquired those skills—if you never learned to brush your teeth, or if you haven't paid your dues at the practice range—then no mental cue in the world is going to be effective.

The cue that works for you will, consequently, depend on your level of experience and the habits you have formed. The goal, you won't be shocked to learn, is complete trust in your skills, so that your entire focus can be on your target. Dr. Bob Rotella tells us that when Nick Price was having his amazing run a couple of years ago, *all* Price thought about when he stood over his ball was his target.

I'm not saying you should turn your conscious mind off: you couldn't if you wanted to. I'm saying that you need to train your conscious mind to get out of the way and avoid introducing tension with a flurry of mental commands.

The ability to play golf is based on repeatable, simple, and good habits formed by the proper use of the instrument—I don't like the word "club"—to make the ball go to the target. Going through a complicated thought process while you're standing over your ball just doesn't work.

The more you concentrate when you're on the playing ground, the worse you're likely to play because your mind is going to be giving orders that interfere with your body's freedom to respond instinctively as an athlete.

Concentrate when you're on the Training Ground—the practice range—because there you are *working* on your game. On the course—the Playing Ground—you should trust your habits and your feel and your athletic instincts.

> **"I've learned to trust the subconscious. My instincts have never lied to me."**
>
> —Tiger Woods

○ ○ ○

WHY DO I CHOKE?

You go to the practice tee fifteen minutes before your tee time. You feel loose, relaxed. Good tempo. Crisp, square contact. Perfect trajectory, consistent distance. You think to yourself, It's going to be a great day.

Then you go to the first tee and slice your drive out-of-bounds right, pull-hook your next ball into the water hazard left, and stumble forward to take your drop—discouraged, demoralized, and wondering what hit you.

Shall I tell you what hit you?

Tension.

Tension—more precisely, excessive muscle tension—is the primary reason for poor execution, regardless of sport or skill. Excessive muscle tension keeps you from learning new skills and from improving on skills you already have. Excessive muscle tension restricts the motor movements necessary for proper execution. Excessive tension short-circuits feel and sensitivity.

That's the conclusion of many sports psychologists, among them Dr. Maynard Howe, a behavioral scientist who has studied golf, golfers, and golf teaching in recent years and who has confirmed what I have learned the hard way in nearly five decades of playing and teaching the game.

The primary cause of excessive tension, says Dr. Howe, is cognitive (mental) interference, which occurs when the golfer is subjected to too much information at the wrong time—that is, just when he's about to hit his ball. Overloaded by too many commands—do this, turn this, drive that—the brain tries to transmit instructions to the muscles, whose response is to tense up.

Mental commands, in effect, paralyze the motor programming process by focusing on the *parts* of the swing rather than the whole. I believe—and this is what I teach, whether I'm teaching Tom Lehman or a twenty-plus handicapper—that a golf swing is a harmonious orchestration of many muscles working together. The pieces can't be broken down and practiced in isolation without extreme detriment to the whole. If you break the golf swing down into its components, you tend to destroy the rhythm, tempo, and fluidity required to execute it.

My point here is that a mechanical approach to the golf swing is the worst possible way to go when you're trying to *play* golf. Don't get me wrong: mechanics *are* important. You need to know how things work. And you need to practice them. But the place to focus on mechanics is on the practice range, not on the golf course. On the golf course, you need some method for screening out cognitive interference if you want your game to improve.

DON'T PLAN AHEAD

A successful business executive has to look ahead—to the coming quarter, the coming year, the coming decade. He has to anticipate. Without strategic planning well into the future, a businessman is dead in the water.

Just the reverse is true for a golfer. The more you look ahead—to the water hazard on the next hole, to that string of tough par fours on the back nine—the more you hurt your chances of making a good swing on the only shot that matters: *this* shot.

Okay, I'll grant you a few exceptions. If you're laying up, you need to think about what kind of shot you want the next one to be. And with a pitch or chip to the green, you need to identify the area you want to be putting from. But aside from that sort of tactical judgment, you should never play ahead of yourself. You should always play in the present tense.

The only thing worse than looking ahead on the golf course is looking backward.

WHY IS GOLF SO DAMN HARD?

Maybe it's because of the complexity of the circuitry in the human nervous system needed to make a seven-ounce club head, multiplied by centrifugal force to a pull of 150 pounds down the shaft at impact, at upward of one hundred miles an hour along a line of tolerance of three degrees either way, make contact on a ball within a tolerance of a tenth of an inch.

Or maybe it's because we haven't gone about it the right way.

GET SMART/SMART

A businessman has to have a smart mind. When he's in the business world competing, he must continuously gather and analyze information, check and recheck assumptions, concentrate. He doesn't want anything to interfere with his conscious control of the situation.

An athlete has to have a smart body. When he's in the arena competing, he wants to let his body and habits control his responses. He doesn't want his conscious mind interfering with his athletic response to the situation.

In golf, you have to have a smart mind *and* a smart body. You need a smart mind for emotional control, for decision making, for all the things that you're getting ready to do. Then you have to be able to use your mind so it doesn't interfere with your body.

But your body needs to be smart, too. It must be trained. It must be flexible and relaxed. It must have the capacity to turn good concepts into good habits.

A golfer can't be smart/dumb or dumb/smart.

A golfer has to be smart/smart.

If as much were written about sex as there has been about golf, life would be extinct by now.

TRAINING VERSUS PLAYING

Correct me if I'm wrong, but your goal is not to get better at *practicing* golf but to get better at *playing* golf, isn't it?

Forgive the sarcasm, but from the way most people approach the game, you'd think they were more interested in working golf than playing it.

One reason for taking students out onto the golf course at the beginning of each Nicklaus-Flick Golf School session should be obvious—they're not having trouble with their practice games, they're having trouble with their golf games.

Let me summarize the differences between what you do on the practice range—the Training Ground—where a good work ethic is appropriate, and the golf course—the Playing Ground—where you need a good play ethic.

TRAINING GROUND	PLAYING GROUND
1. Conscious mind in control.	1. Subconscious mind, habits in control.
2. Respond like a mechanic: find out what's wrong, fix it.	2. Respond like an athlete: create positive image, do it.

TRAINING GROUND	PLAYING GROUND
3. Focus on individual parts of swing.	3. Focus on whole swing.
4. Swing mechanics–oriented.	4. Target-oriented.
5. Analyze.	5. Visualize.
6. Verbalize.	6. Feel.
7. Construct, develop.	7. Execute, play.

WANTED: CONSISTENCY

The very first morning I meet students enrolled in a session of the Nicklaus-Flick Golf School, I always ask each one what he or she most wants to get from the school, what improvements are most desired. Invariably, I hear one or both of two things: more distance, more consistency.

I won't lie to you: distance is number one. Everybody wants to hit the ball farther. The golf equipment industry counts on that. It's like real estate, only instead of location, location, location, the three most important things in golf seem to be distance, distance, distance.

The professionals and better amateurs I work with, on the other hand, seldom talk about getting more distance. Okay, I concede that one reason may be that they already have plenty. But better golfers always list consistency before distance.

So when somebody says he wants to get more distance, I just nod and say fine and start talking about the things he can do to get more distance, and—lo and behold—pretty soon we're talking about ways to be more consistent.

Consistency is the key to just about everything in golf. I don't care what your swing looks like: if you can make it repeat, you can play the game. And I don't care how long you are off the tee—250, 215, 180 yards: if you can make the ball travel in the same direction with the same curvature most of the time, you can play the game.

The following list will help you create consistency. I'm going to talk about each in the next few chapters, but I want you to start thinking about them now. The reason I'm being so pushy is that I believe greater consistency will do more than anything else to enhance your enjoyment in playing the game.

1. A mind-set and a Pre-Shot Routine that create a precise awareness of the target and protect against cognitive interference with the swinging of the golf instrument.
2. Grip pressure that is sensitive to the position of the club face and speed of the club head throughout the swing.
3. Posture and setup that permit the body to respond freely, smoothly, and in balance.
4. Correct aim and body alignment.
5. The club swinging in balance with the target line.
6. A constant spine angle throughout your swing.
7. Good rhythm, smooth tempo.
8. A sequence of moves based on the philosophy of trying to make the club head put the ball in the target area.

IN THE BEGINNING, THERE MUST BE WORDS

Words are important. The words your conscious mind hears and processes have a profound effect on the way your subconscious mind reacts and your body responds.

The challenge of good teaching is to be able to select words that fit the student's needs but that do not interfere with his translation of ideas into actions.

"Power," for instance, is not a good word for the average golfer. Neither is "hit." The former suggests increased effort, the latter an aggressive, snapping blow. Both work in the subconscious to create tension. When the body receives "power" and "hit" messages from the brain, it tenses up for action. That's fine if you're a middle linebacker and the guy across the line in the different-colored jersey has just said, "Hut-one!" It's not fine if you're standing on a tee with a golf club in your hand.

"Club" is another word that I've tried to evict from my golf vocabulary. I haven't succeeded because the word is too solidly rooted in the language of the game, but I much prefer to think of an iron or even a driver as an "instrument." Think about it. If you have an "instrument" in your hand instead of a "club," aren't you a lot less likely to jump out of your shoes trying to smash the ball and a lot more likely to make a smooth swing?

I try to substitute "instrument" for "club" when I'm teaching, but I recognize it's a losing battle. You'll see "instrument" used in the pages that follow to make a special point, but even when I backslide and use "club," I hope you'll be thinking "instrument."

Take the word "takeaway." This, of course, is the common term for the movement of the club away from the ball on the backswing. But I prefer the word "swingaway" because of the important difference—important in my mind, at least—between "take" and "swing." The former suggests abruptness and aggression, the latter fluidity and rhythm. I associate abruptness and aggression with tension and force. I associate fluidity and rhythm with the golf swing.

As with instrument/club, I don't expect to win the swingaway/takeaway battle, but I promise you I'll keep on trying.

"Touch," "sensitivity," "balance," "tempo," and—above all—"feel" are good golf words. You need all these qualities for all your short-game shots—that's obvious enough to anyone who's ever picked up a golf . . . *instrument*. But you also need them in your full-swing shots to achieve distance—which, as every tour professional will tell you, is not the result of a powerful effort but the consequence of effortless power.

DO NO HARM

Perhaps the most compelling part of the Hippocratic oath is where the physician vows to "do no harm." Who can argue with that? Well, I wish there were a Hippocratic oath for golf teachers because I think most golfers—all but professionals and a tiny minority of the rest—have been harmed by the way golf has been taught over the years.

Golf has been taught as an exercise in mechanics, when in fact it is a game of feel. For instance, consider the following set of instructions:

- Keep your head down.
- Keep your left arm straight.
- Make a conscious effort to turn your shoulders.
- Make a conscious effort to shift your weight.
- Make a conscious effort to clear your left hip.
- Drive your legs for power.
- Concentrate for control.

Sound familiar? They should. They form the core of conventional instruction. But individually and collectively they are bad medicine because each produces tension—first in a player's mind, then in his golf swing.

Even worse medicine is the One-Piece Takeaway, which has been prescribed for everybody, willy-nilly, without regard to experience or ability.

Let me make myself crystal clear on this: because of the likelihood—make that near certainty—of its introducing tension into the golf swing, the concept of the One-Piece Takeaway is, in my opinion, the single most harmful idea the average golfer can bring with him to the golf course.

SO WHAT'S WRONG WITH THE ONE-PIECE TAKEAWAY?

Nothing, if it's the consequence of the swinging elements moving together in harmony.

Everything, if it's the consequence of a conscious, mechanical command from mind to body.

What usually happens when the average golfer steps up to his ball thinking OnePieceTakeawayOnePieceTakeawayOnePieceTakeaway, the way so much golf instruction in recent years has conditioned him to do? His shoulders tighten to initiate the backswing, his arms and wrists get rigid in response, and his upper body turns stiffly, pulling the club head way to the inside. The body may get into the right position, but the club ends up too flat and in the wrong position, creating tension in the hands and arms. This triggers a lunge with the shoulders at the change of direction—what I call a rescue mission for a club that's gotten out of position.

In my opinion, the club's gotten out of position primarily because of tension created by a mental command—and *that's* what makes the One-Piece Takeaway, as commonly taught and understood, such a bad idea for most golfers.

It doesn't have to be that way.

If the takeaway occurs as a natural consequence of the hands and arms turning the shoulders, then I would say it is of "one piece." What's missing is the tension created when the mind orders the body to perform a One-Piece Takeaway.

This isn't some idle exercise in semantics. I believe that the distinction I've just drawn is at the core of what needs to be changed about the way the golf swing is taught.

There are three solid reasons for dumping the popular notion of the One-Piece Takeaway:

1. It creates tension in the body that robs the golfer of *feel* for his instrument.
2. It puts the shoulders in charge of the takeaway and the change of direction, thereby destroying the rhythm and sequence of moves in the golf swing.
3. It causes the club head to diverge from its desired arc on the backswing, thereby contributing to an over-the-top move on the forward swing.

But I'm getting a little ahead of myself. In Lessons 5, 6, and 7 I explain what I believe is the *right* way for the average golfer to think about the takeaway . . . excuse me, the *swing-away.*

REMEMBER YOUR GOAL

The goal in golf is not to have a pretty, picture-perfect swing. A lot of mighty-fine golfers have had idiosyncratic swings that no teacher would be foolhardy enough to try to get his students to copy exactly.

Does Ray Floyd have a perfect golf swing? Lee Trevino? Chi Chi Rodriguez? Arnold Palmer? They would be the first to admit that their golf swings don't look much like one of those computer-generated "perfect" swings or what they grew up hearing was a "classic" swing.

Do they have *great* golf swings? You betcha—great for *them.*

A "flaw" becomes a player's "style" when he's able to repeat it and turn it into a habit that lets him control his ball flight.

And I think you'll agree that those guys have done a pretty good job of that.

Golf is an art form, not a science. You don't have to conform to some mechanical model of a perfect swing. You just have to remember your goal—to have a bunch of fun by making a little white ball go from the ground here in front of you into a target area over there.

> **"Tension is an insurmountable barrier to effective motor performance."**
>
> **—Dr. Maynard Howe**

COACH

Over the years, I've worked with thousands of golfers, from rank beginners to the best golfers ever to play the game. Now, I'm pretty good at names, and I seldom forget a golf swing, but half the time or more—and if you've been to one of my schools, you know this is true—I address people as "Coach."

The reason I do that is I want you to *be* your own coach. I'll work with someone for a while, watch him hit some shots, try to crawl inside his mind to see how he's absorbing the things we've talked about, and then I'll say, "Tell me, Coach, what do you feel here? What do you do in this situation? What are you sensing there?"

I want you to participate in this learning experience as a teacher as well as a student. I want you to be able to feel and identify the feedback your own body gives you.

The first step in fixing a problem is correctly identifying its cause. The first time a student, after hitting a bad shot, turns to me and says, "Jim, I know what I did then, I changed grip pressure just as I started down," I know that he's started to become his own coach.

Way to go there, Coach.

SCORECARD SUMMARY

- In golf, as in all sports, excessive tension is the primary reason for poor execution.
- Mental commands paralyze the motor programming process by focusing on *parts* of the swing rather than on the whole.
- Key Concept: *Understand and respect the distinction between Training Ground and Playing Ground.*
- Eight Keys to Consistency:

1. Mind-set and Pre-Shot Routine that protect against cognitive interference with swinging of golf instrument.
2. Grip pressure that is sensitive to position of club face and speed of club head.
3. Posture and setup that permit your body to respond freely, smoothly, and in balance.
4. Correct aim and body alignment.
5. Club swinging in balance with target line.
6. Constant spine angle throughout your swing.
7. Good rhythm, smooth tempo.
8. A sequence of moves based on a philosophy of trying to make club head put ball in target area.

LESSON 3

FROM GREEN TO TEE

IF A GOLFER COMES to me and says he wants to restructure his swing and rebuild his golf game completely, the first place I take him is to the green—and not just because thirty-six strokes on a par seventy-two course are intended to be made with a putter.

The larger reason is that the green is the best point of departure for learning the basics of the game, from aim to Pre-Shot Routine to posture to grip pressure to the essential pendulum-like swing. Aside from the instrument employed, the main difference between the putt and the drive is the distance required of the swing.

That's why learning to play golf from green to tee can be so valuable. By starting on the green and working back to the tee, you experience—and you *feel*—a couple of important principles that would have seemed more abstract had you started on the tee:

- The distance to the target determines the length of the swing.

- The length of the swing determines the amount of the pivot.

My point is that a mechanical approach makes the turning of the shoulders, the driving of the hips, the conscious effort to accelerate the body's movement, and so on the *cause* of the club moving.

They are not the cause. They are the *result* of the club moving. And that's a big, big difference.

Do not use your body to move the club. Let your body *respond* to the moving of the club.

A LITTLE Q & A

Mind if I ask you a few questions?

No, Jim, go right ahead.

Fine. Here's the first one: do you pivot when you putt?

When I putt? Of course not! What kind of a silly question is that?

Sorry, no offense intended. Most people have exactly the same reaction because the answer is so obvious. You move your putter with your hands, arms, and shoulders. The goal is to keep the putter on line, face square, and under control. The truth is that, when you're on the green, it does not require much effort in the movement of the club to get the ball to the hole no matter the length of the putt. The distance doesn't require a pivot.

Now, do you pivot when you chip?

Hmm, yes, I guess. A little.

Right. But I suspect you don't make a conscious effort to pivot. For a low-trajectory shot from a few feet up to fifteen to twenty yards off the green, you just swing the club back a little more, whatever amount's needed to reach the target, and your shoulders are turned by the extra swinging effort, causing a slight pivot. The pivot results from the swinging of your arms and the use of your club to make the ball go into the target area. The body doesn't turn the club. The use of the club turns the body.

Okay.

Now, do you pivot when you pitch?

Yes, sure, a little more than for a chip.

But you don't make a conscious effort to pivot more . . .

No, not really.

Let's hope so. If your mind is tied up in how to turn your shoulders or to pivot, you don't have as much feel for how the club is swinging or how long the swing is. For a high-trajectory shot from near the green, it's the length of the swing, determined by the distance the ball needs to travel, that causes the pivot.

Okay, I have one last question: do you pivot when you hit your driver?

When I hit my driver? Of course I do! What kind of silly question is that? I turn my shoulders, I anchor my right leg, I start my forward swing with my left hip, I clear my left side, I drive my . . .

Oh, so that's your problem.

PUTTING AND PICTURES

Good players play golf by pictures and by feel. What I mean by that is they see a picture of the ball going to the target—and they associate a feel with exactly what it is that makes that picture happen. When they hit a good shot it reinforces a positive habit that makes possible the *next* good shot. My job as a teacher is simple: to help you see those pictures and experience that feel. That way, when you make a good shot, you can use the experience to develop positive habits.

Take the shoulder turn. When I try *consciously* to turn, my shoulders tend to tighten up. Conscious mental direction creates physical tension. But when my setup is correct, and when I just let my arms swing, free and easy, back and forth, in a nice rhythm, they turn my upper body effortlessly and efficiently. I get a full turn, but not by *trying* to turn. My turn occurs naturally and without conscious effort as a consequence of the swinging of my club.

That's why a good place to begin learning about the full swing is on the green. It's easier to get a complete mental picture of the shot, it's easier to learn to hold the target in your mind during the swing, and it's easier to experience what it feels like when the club face comes in contact with the ball. It's also easier to ingrain the notion that it's the swinging force of the club head that gives the ball the energy to get to the target area—and, consequently, it's the length of the swing rather than effort level that determines how far the ball travels.

Because the green has so many variables—fast, slow, uphill, downhill, sidehill, against the grain, with the grain, cross-grained—when you work on putting, you're working on the sensitivity, feel, and creativity that is needed all over the golf course.

That's why it's easier to take what you learn on the green and around the green to the tee than it is to start with the full swing—with its implicit expectation of force and power—and bring that to the green.

FINGERS SECURE, ARMS RELAXED

The green is where a person begins to relate to the game in a manner that lets him play golf. The best way to learn the game is by feeling the sensitivity required for short shots, then build to the full swing.

Start by identifying the grip pressure that lets you feel the weight of the club head. Now feel the swinging force of the club head. As it comes down and strikes the ball, let your hands and arms become aware of the minimum amount of tension that is really required for solid contact.

Do this and you'll begin to sense the desirable amount of sensitivity in your hands and forearms. Become aware of how light your arms can be. What you're looking for is "Fingers Secure, Arms Relaxed."

Sounds simple, but it's really a difficult concept. I guess it goes back to our caveman heritage: put a blunt instrument in a man's hands, and he immediately starts looking for something to smash. If you're trying to cave in a saber-toothed tiger's skull as an alternative to being eaten, then the concept of "grip it and rip it" makes some sense. Worrying too much about grip pressure at a time like that might be counterproductive.

But while Fingers Secure, Arms Relaxed may not be relevant in handling tiger attacks, I guarantee you it's the best way to deal with a golf ball. You want your fingers to stay around the club. You don't want them to separate during the swing. But you want your arms to have the freedom to respond to the weight of the club.

What I like to see is a pendulum-like putting stroke, where the amount of backswing is fairly compatible with roughly the same amount of forward swing.

Note that I said "compatible," not "identical," not to mention "fairly" and "roughly." It's not that I'm trying to be cagey. It's that golf is an art, not a science. The truth is, if an actual pendulum is swinging in an arc, and if we sneak a ball in front of it on the forward swing, then the resistance supplied by the ball is going to shorten the forward swing.

What that means is you shouldn't *try* to accelerate to create a forward swing that's exactly equal in distance to the backswing. The effort to accelerate changes grip pressure, which in turn creates tension in the forearms, which in turn overrides the pendulum-like motion you were trying to create in the first place.

Deceleration is bad. But a slightly shorter forward swing isn't a sign of deceleration; it's a sign that the laws of physics are in good working order. When a swinging force meets resistance—if only from a ball weighing less than two ounces—it's going to slow down. Period. An extra effort to increase your acceleration at impact undermines the whole idea of the pendulum-like stroke.

Let the laws of physics handle things. After all, they've been at it a little longer than we have.

SOFT SELL

The basic elements of putting—aim, setup, routine, visualization, solid contact, square contact, pendulum-like stroke—all carry over into the full swing not as isolated parts of a mechanical process, but as seamlessly integrated components of a graceful, fluid, athletic movement.

Is putting about violent action? Even a novice golfer knows the answer to that question. Put a putter in his hands and ask him to move the ball a mere twenty feet and he's not going to rock back on his heels and swing with all his might.

Is it about smoothness and rhythm? For a true novice trying to knock one in from twenty feet, the first putt will usually be an abrupt, wristy hit that sends the ball twenty feet past the target. The second putt, usually an overadjustment to the first, will come up five feet short. After a couple of putts, he'll answer yes, it's all about smoothness and rhythm, even if he's not certain how to achieve either.

Is it about listening to the music? *What?* Now, wait a minute . . .

Okay, maybe I'm rushing our hypothetical novice a little. But I'm going to have a lot better chance of getting him to hear the music of golf a lot quicker if we start out on the green and work backward to the tee.

SCORECARD SUMMARY

- Length of shot determines length of swing.
- Length of swing determines amount of pivot.
- Length of swing rather than effort determines distance.
- Key Concept: *Fingers Secure, Arms Relaxed.*

LESSON 4

A GAME OF FEEL

THE FIVE BEST GOLFERS ever to play the game are, in my opinion, Jack Nicklaus, Ben Hogan, Bobby Jones, Sam Snead, and Byron Nelson. No doubt there can be some heated, nineteenth-hole argument about what order they should be listed in, but I think most people agree that those names belong on the Top 5 list.

Now, these golfers have radically different swings—no two could ever be confused with each other:

- Jack Nicklaus grew up on a Donald Ross course in Ohio, where he developed a swing that created a high, soft ball flight.
- Growing up in Texas, Ben Hogan needed a ball that would bore underneath the wind, so he had a swing that created a low ball flight with a lot of hook, at least at first.
- Bobby Jones didn't play with a dynamic, aggressive golf swing because the equipment in his day wouldn't allow it: he had a soft, sweeping swing and even occasionally

let go of the club with his left hand at the top of his swing to keep from stressing his hickory shaft.

- Sam Snead had a much stronger body than Jones and could afford a more aggressive approach after steel shafts were introduced. His swing was similar to Jones's but more upright because it fit his long arms and body type.
- Byron Nelson fought a shank early in his career: he developed a swing that dropped the club inside the backswing arc when coming down, and he used his feet and legs to support the club from the inside to eliminate the over-the-top attack that could produce an occasional shank.

Different folks, different strokes.

Now, I'm not suggesting you copy any of their swings. I'm not suggesting you copy *anyone's* swing for that matter. What I am suggesting is that you take careful note of the one thing, besides their incredible competitive spirit, that these great golfers have in common: they are all *feel* players who learned to use the golf club to make the ball go to the target.

Would your next five include Arnold Palmer, Lee Trevino, Tom Watson, Gary Player, Nick Faldo, Walter Hagen, Gene Sarazen, Greg Norman? Maybe, maybe not. Doesn't matter. You'd get the same result: no two swings alike, all feel players.

The only message the golf ball understands is what the club face tells it to do. If all you do is work on mechanics, your mechanical golf movements may improve, but your ability to control the golf club won't. You might become master of the "turn-my-shoulders-drive-my-hips-twist-my-body" school of thought, but the last time I looked, that wasn't a game. If you spend time learning how to use the club, how to *feel* it, you will be learning to *play* golf.

ONE SIZE DOES *NOT* FIT ALL

The depersonalization of contemporary society comes across a lot in golf instruction today. Everybody gets put in the same hopper. One swing fits all. Learn by the numbers. Connect the dots. Fit your own unique mix of physical abilities, body characteristics, and mental makeup to a single approach, as if there were only one. Conform to a computer-generated model of a "perfect" golf swing.

That makes me madder than hell.

The minute you start restricting people from doing and being what they can, given their own innate abilities and makeup, you're going down the wrong path. That's true in life. And it's true in golf.

You don't cut the golfer to fit the pattern.

You cut the pattern to fit the golfer.

WHAT IS *FEEL*?

Your mind precisely identifies what your body experiences. That's a fact. But is your mind a constant? No. And neither is your body. One day you might feel relaxed, in balance, focused. Another day you might be tense, out of sync, distracted. You have to adapt. The trick is to get your mind and body on the same page, to make adjustments to get today's body and today's mind in harmony.

To do that on a golf course, you have to have a sense of feel.

The golfing public has, in the last few decades, been steered away from golf as a game of feel. The emphasis today is on the mechanics of the swing. As you may have already noticed, I think this is the wrong path.

Here and throughout this book, I will return again and again to the idea of *feel* in golf because I believe, based on a lifetime of teaching and observing great players, that feel is the very soul of the game.

WHY THINKING ISN'T ENOUGH

Precise identification of what's right and what's wrong, what works and what doesn't work, is the key first step to improvement in most human endeavors.

Most of the time this is an essentially (if not exclusively) mental exercise: you collect information, you evaluate it, you develop a plan, you act.

Not in golf.

You can't assume that just because you issue a mental command your body is going to execute it. Words—mine or anybody else's—only take you so far. And you don't exactly have the best vantage point for observing your golf swing. You need to *feel* what's going on to be able to identify precisely what works and what doesn't and what needs to be done.

That's why I talk so much to students on the practice range about feeling their club head. Unless you're surrounded by mirrors, you can't see where it is at every moment during the golf swing. But you can feel where it is. In my opinion, you *must* feel where it is if you are to reach your full potential as a golfer.

The more you draw on your sense of feel, the better chance you have of precisely identifying what's going on in your golf swing. And the more precisely you identify what's right and what's wrong, the better chance you have of making corrections and making your swing repeat.

Your hands are the passageway for feel between your body and the club head.

THE LONG AND THE SHORT OF IT

What is the difference between a swing that produces a delicate 60-yard pitch shot and one that delivers a booming 275-yard drive?

Not much.

One key message I want to deliver—and, believe me, I will deliver it over and over again until you accept it as the truth—is that the basic concepts underlying the short game and the full swing are essentially the same.

Your swing doesn't change very much when you go from a sixty-yard part shot to a full swing from the tee—it mainly just gets longer to accommodate the instrument being used and the distance the ball has to travel.

Are there *any* differences? Sure. Do they involve radical departures in aim, posture, routine, or relationship between the swinging and turning elements? No.

That's one of the reasons I like to start players with the short game: because it helps them develop the imagery to play golf, along with feel and sensitivity for the use of the club and the swinging elements.

For instance, when you're making a part shot—say, a sixty-yard pitch—it's easier to sense the swinging force of the club head and the position of the club face than it is in a full swing with a long iron or a wood.

To develop your sense of *feel* in golf, put down your driver and pick up a short or middle iron.

WHICH END IS UP?

Whenever I hear people say that "the golf swing is controlled by the big muscles" or that "golf is a big-muscle game," I look to see if they have a special place for attaching a golf club to their hips or their shoulders. Maybe I'm missing something somewhere, but the only parts of my body that touch my golf club are my hands—more specifically, my fingers.

Our fingers need to help us sense where the club face is through the whole golf swing. They can't do that if their position and pressure on the grip don't allow them to feel the weight of the club. If your hands can't give you correct information about what's going on with your instrument, how are you going to develop into a feel player? You're not.

Try something for me. Stand up, hold a club straight out parallel to the floor, and close your eyes. Better still, have someone hand you the club after your eyes are closed. Now twist the club around and try to identify precisely which way the club face is pointing—up, down, left, right, whatever.

A good player can sense exactly where the face of that club is pointing at all times. It's a matter of awareness for the instrument. It's a matter of feel.

> **"Golf is a game of motion and rhythm, not of position and mechanics."**
>
> **—Martin Hall**

USE YOUR IMAGINATION

Rigid rules, the "Thou shalts" and "Thou shalt nots" of how to swing a golf club, are the enemy of feel. To help develop feel in your golf swing, use your imagination.

Try using the same club for a variety of shots—or the "wrong" club on purpose.

Try playing nine holes with just a five iron and a putter.

Try putting with your three wood.

Try playing a round taking at least one more club than the yardage would otherwise call for on every shot (except off the tee and on the green).

(Please, *please* do not try the reverse—that is, using one less club and swinging extra hard. You'd be better off giving up golf.)

Let's say you're sixty yards from a green that is equally receptive to a low shot that lands a little short of the green and runs to the hole or a lofted shot that carries all the way to the flagstick.

Nobody's behind you, you're playing by yourself—why not try both?

For the low-trajectory shot, you want to grip your club a fraction tighter because you want to keep the grip end out in front through impact. You don't want the club head to pass your hands. You don't want to be wristy. So your grip pressure will be just a fraction tighter in your top hand.

For the high pitch shot, you want to hold your club with a lighter grip. You want to let the club head swing fully through the ball. You want the club face to sweep the ball rather than pinch it against the turf. So your grip pressure will be just a fraction lighter in your left hand.

Which club? Hey, if we were partners playing for a big two-dollar Nassau, I'd be happy to offer an opinion. But this is an exercise in imagination. You've got a whole bagful there—you pick the club. Or several clubs. Find out how they affect the ball's flight to the target.

Find out how they *feel*.

○ ○ ○

DON'T CONFUSE THE INABILITY TO EXECUTE WITH THE INABILITY TO UNDERSTAND

Every now and then, someone in a school session will say, "Well, I don't understand that."

My usual answer, unless I'm having a bad day and realize I'm being particularly obtuse, is what Peter Kostis, an old colleague at the *Golf Digest* schools, used to say: "Don't confuse the inability to execute with the inability to understand."

And I go on: "You understand the material very well. Right now you haven't done it often enough that you can execute it. So don't try to get more material. Spend more time on execution."

I'm not trying to be harsh. I'm trying to be realistic. You learn golf the way you learn everything else: step by step. Get too much all at once and you break down from information overload.

Let's say you're a grown-up and you decide to study French. Do you go to school for a semester and then one day wake up speaking the language perfectly? No! You practice, you absorb, you learn in stages. Golf is exactly like learning a language: there's a huge gap between intellectual understanding and physical feel. You bridge that gap with repeated execution. In other words, practice.

WHAT HIT ME?

Bright, sunshiny day, and you have the club swinging in a simple, in-balance arc. The trajectory and shape of your shots are consistent. All's right with the world. Your swing *feels* right.

Then something happens. The nice draw you've been hitting becomes a pull-hook. Or the full-bodied fade that's worked so well mutates into a banana slice. A dream round turns into a nightmare. *Nothing* feels right.

Sound familiar? Trust me: we've all been there.

Things were going good, suddenly they're going bad—how do I get my swing back in balance? To answer that, you have to be able to feel—then understand—what went haywire in the first place.

Here's one scenario. The body runs forward prematurely. The weight of the club falls back and out of position. The grip end gets where the club head can't catch up. The arms take an outside-in route because the chest is blocking their way. All this results in an abrupt, desperate, last-instant rotation of the wrists (the pull-hook) or an open club face striking the ball from an outside-in path (the slice).

The precise diagnosis is not the issue here—there are other things that cause a swing to go out of balance. What's important is that in order to *understand* what happened, you first have to *feel* what happened.

You have to have freedom of movement in your hands, arms, and shoulders as you swing your club through the golf ball. And you have to be able to sense when that freedom becomes constrained or compromised.

We all go through our own trial-and-error period trying to get our understanding and physical execution levels in sync. You can't do it by the thinking process alone. That doesn't give you the in-depth sense of what you're doing. The soul's not there.

To *play* golf, you need to *feel* golf.

"The goal is effortless power, not a powerful effort."

—Bob Toski

LET THE EYES HAVE IT

Players from the Jones, Snead, and Hogan eras measured distance with their eyes. How far is it to the green? Oh, a hard five iron or maybe an easy four.

In today's game, distances are laser-measured and marked: golfers have come to expect every sprinkler head to tell them exactly how far it is to the center of the green. Some courses give you front edge and back edge as well. A lot of courses have fairway disks at 200, 150, and 100 yards. Even courses that haven't gone to the expense of a full-scale laser measurement have 150-yard markers.

The rationale for this is to speed up play. The argument—and I'm not certain I buy it—is that a golfer who knows precisely how far it is to the pin won't spend as much time deciding on which club to use.

But I'm not sure that all this measuring and marking hasn't cost the average player something in learning to trust his eyes and in developing his feel for the game.

As a test, try playing nine holes without once looking at a sprinkler head. (I don't suppose you can avoid looking at the 150-yard markers.) Make your club selection based on what your eyes tell you. Keep track of the times you over-club and under-club. My prediction, for golfers who play enough to know their game, is that more often than you think, you will pull just the right club.

That could give new meaning to the phrase "Seeing is believing."

Conscious work on mechanics should be done on the Training Ground, not on the Playing Ground.

"GOLF IS A GAME OF EMOTION AND ADJUSTMENTS"

Jack Nicklaus said that to me in 1990, the year we started to work together. He was talking about how so many younger players on the tour today have a very mechanical golf swing. His point was that mechanics can only take you so far. If you can't feel what's happening to your mind and body when you're on the golf course, then you can't make those necessary adjustments to play the shot that's called for at the time.

This is especially true in competition, where frequent adjustments may be called for. On a par five protected by water, do you go for the green on your second shot or lay up? It depends. If it's Sunday afternoon and you're just off the lead, you probably go for it. If you're the leader, maybe not. And all options shift if it's Friday, not Sunday, and you're trying to make the cut.

What happens if you discover on the third hole of your all-important regular Saturday morning match—two-dollar Nassau with automatic presses, plus one-dollar greenies and sandies—that you left your "A" swing back in the parking lot? You make adjustments. You figure out a way to play with what you have that particular day. "I've won with a lot of different swings," Jack once told me. "Sometimes I've won not because I've had my best swing, but because I used the club better than anyone else that week."

Nobody who's ever played golf has been better than Jack Nicklaus at assessing a competitive situation and making on-course adjustments. Often it means going against the adrenaline flow. If Jack is in contention, particularly in a major, he becomes so conservative in his club selection that, if he mishits it, the damage will be minimal. Other times, he can be so bold it seems foolhardy—until you see the result.

That may not seem relevant to most golfers. After all, we're not likely to be playing for a green jacket in this lifetime. But it is relevant to everybody's approach to the game (and, while we're on the subject, to life). After all, each of us has some goal every time we step on the golf course, whether it is shooting par, breaking eighty, carding a personal best, or getting on the good side of one hundred.

ALL FOR ONE, ONE FOR ALL

Your body and your club must be in harmony. If you take an overly mechanical approach to the golf swing, you tend to think about your hips and shoulders and arms as separate units that move independent of your club. But body parts should move in harmony with and support of the club. If you learn to feel where the club is and how fast it's moving, then your body parts gravitate back to the speed of the club rather than outrace or attempt to power the club.

THE MOZART WITHIN

Take this big club and go hit that little ball as far as you can.

Put it that way, no wonder the caveman impulse takes over our bodies on the golf course.

The problem is, if we want to have half a chance of hitting a golf ball a long way, we need to suppress the caveman instinct and let the Mozart in us come out. We need to overcome the impulse to brutalize the ball and instead develop a habit of letting the swing sweep the club head through the ball.

Think of it this way: there's no need to *hit* anything.

If the club head is swinging smoothly and freely, and if the ball gets in its path, everything else will take care of itself.

> **"You train with mechanics. You play by feel."**
> —Jack Nicklaus

LITTLE COREY AND LONG JOHN

Most golfers are interested in two things: more distance and/or more consistency.

Now, not everybody can have great length. Corey Pavin wouldn't be one of the best players in the world if success in golf were based on length.

Also, length is only one factor in the golf equation: John Daly wouldn't have won two majors if he couldn't putt.

Does that mean Daly, who could also hit the ball farther than anybody on the tour until Tiger Woods came along, is going to have a better career than Pavin?

Personally, I think not. Even though he has won two major championships, I don't think Daly, big hitter and good putter that he is, has the course management skills and ball flight control to continue to compete consistently under all conditions. He may develop that consistency; I hope he does.

Pavin, on the other hand, has marvelous feel, as much as anybody playing today. He has every shot in the book—and some that haven't been written down—*except* the 300-yard drive.

TOM WATSON'S FEEL TEST

When Tom Watson thinks that he's lost his feel for the weight in the club head, he turns the club upside down, grabs the shaft just below the club head in his hands, and makes some swings. The shaft swinging through the air feels very light. Then, when he turns the club back to the correct position, he's able to feel the heavy weight of the club head. Tom's even been known to do this on the golf course. That's how important it is for him to feel the weight of the club head in his swing.

SNEAD OIL

Sam Snead used to talk about how he wanted his swing to feel "oily." He wanted a sense that there was nothing locked up when he was swinging, that his whole body was very free.

Sam also used to hit a lot of golf balls barefoot. He said it helped him feel how his feet were responding and working in harmony with his swing.

Maybe you should try it. Be careful, though: when the Dress Code Police come to write you a summons, I'm not sure it will help to tell them you're just trying to get oily.

Given a choice between great rhythm and mediocre mechanics, or great mechanics and mediocre rhythm, *all* good golfers would choose great rhythm.

○ ○ ○

"FEEL THE CLUB HEAD"

That's almost the first thing out of my mouth on the first session at a Nicklaus-Flick Golf School; it's one of the last things I say during the last session, and in between I say it so often it comes to sound more like a chant. A student once told me he was going to have letterhead stationery printed up for me with no name, no address, no telephone number, just the phrase "Feel the Club Head" on the top. "Everybody would know it was you, Jim," he said.

All I can do is plead guilty as charged: I do believe that feeling the club head is the starting point of a good golf swing.

The inner workings of the human mind are way beyond my training and expertise. And I sure don't try to hypnotize people, so I can't say I try to plant a posthypnotic suggestion. I guess you'd call "Feel the Club Head" an *instead-of*-hypnotic suggestion.

Whatever you call it, the point of "Feel the Club Head" is to get your mind, body, and club working as one. During the golf swing, you need to be able to feel where your club head is and how fast it's going. You can't do that if your muscles are tense. I never tell people to "slow down," which can cause deceleration and choppy tempo. I tell them instead to "Feel the Club Head." You can't do that unless your muscles are relaxed, as relaxed muscles contribute to a steady tempo.

Trying to overpower the ball and trying to overcontrol the club have the same effect—they tighten you up. If tension is the number one barrier to a consistent golf swing, and I believe it is, then "feeling the club head" is the number one requirement for eliminating tension and developing a consistent golf swing.

At least it is in my book.

SCORECARD SUMMARY

- Basic concepts underlying the short game and the full swing are essentially the same.
- To develop a sense of feel, work on short-game shots.
- Bridge the gap between understanding and feel with repeated execution.
- Effortless power, not powerful effort.
- Work on swing mechanics should be done on the Training Ground, not on the Playing Ground.
- Key Concept: *"Feel the Club Head" to get mind, body, and instrument working as one.*

LESSON 5

GRAVITY, TWO PENDULUMS, AND THE GOLF SWING

NO ONE LEFT A greater legacy to golf than Bobby Jones. He stood for all that is best about the game. He set standards of excellence, respect for the game, and just plain class that few have even approached. Possessor of a marvelously fluid golf swing and a fierce competitive spirit, he dominated his era and set a performance mark—his famous Grand Slam—that will never be equaled.

But, more pertinent for our purposes, he also bequeathed—albeit inadvertently—a key to the golf swing that could change your life. Or at least the part of it you spend on a golf course.

Some years ago a scientist named Dr. David Williams conducted a research project based on a videotape (transferred from an instructional film made in the 1930s) of Bobby Jones hitting golf balls. Williams fed the videotape into a biomechanical computer, which permitted him to conduct a variety of measurements of Jones's swing. Williams published his findings in a book entitled *The Science of the Golf Swing*.

I think the results will amaze you. I know they excited me. Moreover, they provided scientific corroboration of an approach to the golf swing that I have been teaching for many years.

The tape shows Jones hitting with his driver 250 to 260 yards. Williams, focusing on the speed of Jones's swing, calculated that from the top of his backswing to the point of contact with his ball Jones's hands and arms were accelerating at a rate of just over thirty-four feet per second per second.

What makes that interesting is that if you were to extend your arm and drop a golf ball, its acceleration rate as it fell to Mother Earth would be just over thirty-two feet per second per second. See where I'm going with this? It means that in the beautiful golf swing that propelled a ball 260 yards with a hickory-shafted driver, the great Bobby Jones did only a little more than let his arms fall out of the sky.

Bobby Jones depended on gravity to build his golf swing.

No, I'm not telling you that if next Saturday you stand up on the first tee, announce, "I'm going to do the 'gravity swing,' " and drop your arms, your ball will go 260 yards. You must have a hinge, and you have to tap into centrifugal force.

Jones did have a hinge—a couple of them—and he did make great use of centrifugal force. But he didn't exactly jump out of his shoes trying to slug the ball: his hands and arms were accelerating at a rate only slightly faster than gravity's pull. And yet at impact his club head was traveling at 165 feet per second per second—or *113 miles an hour.*

That's why I want to sell you on the idea of developing a pendulum-like swing, one where you let your arms swing free and generate club-head speed without a lot of extra effort.

Why not get maximum benefit from the most consistent force in nature before trying to improve on it?

○ ○ ○

> **"The club weighs less than a pound. The ball weighs less than two ounces. We don't need to prepare for violence."**
>
> **—Bob Toski**

NEWS FLASH! LAW OF GRAVITY CONFIRMED!

Want to do a little scientific experiment with me?

Stand up, hold your arms out parallel to the ground, relaxed and loose, and let them fall to your sides.

Okay, hold them out there again, only this time clench your fists as though you were strangling a three iron. Now let your arms fall to your sides.

Definitely slower the second time, right?

Congratulations, you have just proved that the law of gravity is still operative—and that it works more efficiently than tensed, locked-up muscles.

Think about that the next time you try to generate more club-head speed by squeezing the club in a vicelike grip, tensing your biceps, and swinging as hard as you can. If you just let your arms free-fall during the golf swing, you can get all sorts of speed out on the end of your club. It's when you *try* really hard to generate speed that you come up short.

Tension destroys any hope of making regular, consistent, and efficient use of your instrument—the golf club. Tension dramatically reduces club-head speed. The less tension you have in your arms, the more gravity becomes your friend.

And remember—gravity alone, if not interfered with, generates almost as much club-head speed as Bobby Jones.

PENDULUM \'pen-jə-ləm\ *n* [NL, fr. L, neut. of *pendulus*] (1600) 1: a body [e.g., a club head] suspended from a fixed point [e.g., a pair of shoulder sockets] so as to swing freely to and fro under the action of gravity and commonly used to regulate movements (as of clockwork) [or as of a golf ball in flight] 2: something (as a state of affairs) that alternates between opposites [i.e., the top of the backswing and the finish]

—*Merriam Webster's Collegiate Dictionary* (slightly amended)

THE PENDULUM-LIKE SWING

The first time I talk to students about the pendulum-like swing I see a lot of skepticism in their eyes. Some of it disappears after our first short-game session because the stroke for the basic clip and pitch shots is certainly pendulum-like and the square contact "feels" right. But the unspoken—and sometimes spoken—reaction is, "Okay. A pendulum's fine, but I'm not going to hit my ball far enough."

And I have to convince you that you will.

The term is "pendulum-like," as in similar (but not identical) to a pendulum. Unlike a true pendulum on a grandfather's clock, of course, the golf swing doesn't keep going back and forth, back and forth, through the same arc indefinitely. But if we examine the properties of how a pendulum swings and then liken it to golf motion, you'll see a lot of similarities.

For most golfers, the pendulum-like swing is the simplest, quickest way to achieve consistent repetition of motion—the much coveted, much pursued, always elusive Repeating Swing.

Attach a golf ball to a string, let it hang from a fixed point, get it swinging, and—presto!—a demonstration pendulum. Question number one, Is there any acceleration? The answer is yes: pendulums accelerate as long as they're swinging down. There is a bottom point—actually, in physics I believe it's called the zero point—where there is no more acceleration. But that is also the point where you've got maximum velocity.

How good is that? You've got your club head picking up speed, picking up speed, then hitting *maximum* speed at contact. That would actually be an optimum transfer of energy.

Next, almost always, comes a question that—*invariably*—sends one of my teaching colleagues, Martin Hall, up the wall, off the charts, and into orbit: "If the pendulum stops picking up speed, that means I have to make sure to accelerate and follow through, right?"

Now, everyone has his hot-button issue. Mine is "One-Piece Takeaway." For Martin, who's one of six members of my staff listed among *Golf* magazine's Top 100 Teachers in America, the thing that drives him craziest is "accelerate and follow through."

Listen to him on the subject:

I can't think of anything worse to try to do with a golf club in your hands than "accelerate and follow through."

Does the swing accelerate? Yes. What's making it accelerate? Gravity. Let me repeat: it's accelerating because of the pull of gravity.

Now, is there a follow-through? Of course there is. Why? Because of the swing, because of momentum.

So with the pendulum-like swing, we have acceleration, and we have follow-through as a consequence of momentum. If you think "accelerate and follow through" when you swing, then you are going to try to help momentum.

Believe me, momentum doesn't need any help.

Martin's right. There is a follow-through in the golf swing, but it's caused by momentum, not a conscious effort. If you go into the golf swing thinking about accelerating at impact to create a big follow-through, you'll undermine the principle of the pendulum-like swing, inevitably cause your muscles to tense up, and almost certainly disrupt the swing's arc with the midpoint increase in effort, thereby reducing the likelihood of a square club face at impact.

Not only that, but you will really annoy Martin Hall.

NOT ONE, BUT TWO

There are actually two pendulums at work. The first is formed by the hands and wrists cocking, uncocking, and recocking. The second is created by the forearms and upper arms swinging from the shoulder sockets.

My former colleague from *Golf Digest* school days Peter Kostis called them the first swing and the second swing. I think of them as two pendulums.

What permits the two pendulums to work together is the combination of the weight in club head, centrifugal force, the good old law of gravity—and the golfer. These pendulums supply about 80 percent of the distance in your golf shot—provided the swinging elements of your body drive the turning elements and not vice versa.

If your grip pressure is too tight, the weight at the end of the club is restricted from doing its job.

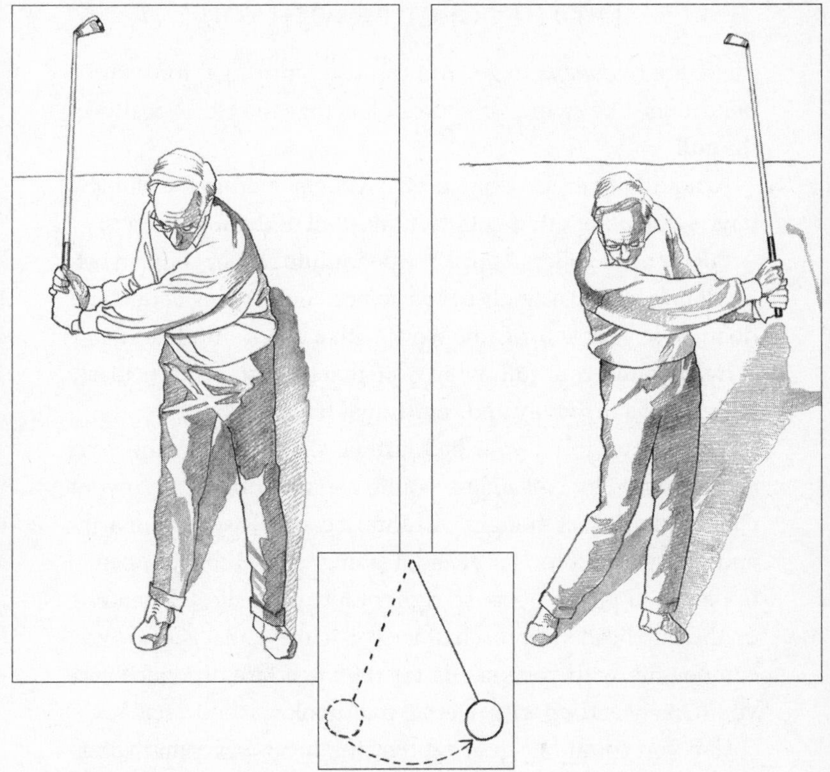

The Pendulum-like Swing. Note the position of the arms midway through the backswing and midway through the forward swing after impact. Identical? No, but close—as in pendulum-like.

If you try consciously to turn your shoulders and shift your weight, you destroy the natural harmony of those two pendulums.

If you try to accelerate at impact and follow through, well, you know what happens there.

But if your posture is good, and your grip pressure—fingers secure, arms relaxed—is correct, you give those two pendulums a chance to work in harmony.

LET THE FORCE BE WITH YOU

There are two ways to go. You can use centrifugal force and a pendulum-like swing, or you can leverage the club—really *hit* the ball.

Arnold Palmer has done pretty well leveraging the club. So have some other good golfers, almost all of them pros.

But for most golfers, I think the pendulum concept offers a better chance for consistently solid contact. You're going to putt and do most of your short-game work with a pendulum-like swing. Why not build your full swing from that head start? Particularly since you have gravity and centrifugal force on your side.

If you want to hit your ball farther, should you swing your arms faster? No. Not unless you're certain you can keep your club head up. That thought will almost certainly send your arms and grip end out too far ahead, leaving your club face open at impact, and produce a push right or a banana slice, depending on the club head's approach to the ball. Unless, that is, you overcompensate with your hands for the open face, in which case you'll likely end up with a lethal pull-hook.

Can you count on squaring the club head with hand action if the grip end of your club gets too far out in front? Not consistently. There just aren't enough nanoseconds for your hands to react.

Your golf club is designed so that the head will square itself if allowed to. But it can't if your grip is too tight, your wrists are stiff, there's too much tension in your shoulders, and your arms aren't soft enough for your left arm to fold easily after impact. You *must* have correct grip pressure—Fingers Secure, Arms Relaxed—so that the club head can build up speed and square itself at impact.

Remember: Bobby Jones's *arms* weren't moving much faster than if he'd just let them drop, but his *club head* was moving at

113 miles an hour. Why? Because of what his hands were doing to tap into the power of centrifugal force.

DON'T TRY HARDER

Everybody tries harder when the chips are down. That's great in the last few minutes of the Super Bowl or the NBA Finals. You want your adrenaline pumping, you want your effort level at maximum. The harder you try, the better your chance of breaking through for a first down or grabbing that offensive rebound.

It doesn't work that way in golf. You think to yourself, I have to hit this shot *hard*, and all that does is produce tension, which dramatically reduces your chances of hitting it *well*.

THE HEARTBEAT OF THE GOLF SWING

Go to a practice green, throw down a ball, and putt it toward the hole—with your driver. Works pretty good, doesn't it? You'll even see a pro use his driver on the green occasionally, generally after he's "lost" his putter in a pond (or snapped it over his knee) on the preceding hole. But that's not my point.

Now take the same driver, tee a ball up, and hit it down the fairway. What's the difference in the two shots? If you answered "About two hundred and fifty yards," you'd be right. But that's not my point, either.

The essential difference between the two shots—and this *is* my point—is that the first employs one pendulum, the second two. And bridging the difference is the cocking, uncocking, and recocking of the wrists—what I call "the heartbeat of the golf swing."

Your arms have to transport the club back and forth. Your body has to respond by turning and supporting this swinging action. But correct hand action is the heartbeat of the golf swing: you must have, through impact, the hand action that creates the club-face position you need for the ball flight you want.

Advanced golfers have less active hands, but the average golfer needs to feel the release of the club head in the cocking-uncocking-recocking of the hands and wrists. That's why, in teaching people the Developmental Swing, I emphasize an early cocking of the wrists. The sooner you learn to feel the role

Ker-*thump*... Ker-*thump*... Ker-*thump*. The cocking, uncocking, and recocking of the wrists give life to the golf swing.

your hands play in the golf swing, the sooner you can count on them to perform as they react to the weight in the club head.

Eight out of ten golfers—and that may be a conservative estimate—have utterly inadequate hand action in their golf swings. That's understandable, considering that they've had it drilled into them that "golf is a big-muscle game" and that they must have a One-Piece Takeaway. As translated by the average golfer, this becomes a prescription for locked-up shoulders, rigid arms, and a mechanical pass at the ball that makes woefully inadequate use of gravity and centrifugal force, the golfer's two best friends.

For the second of the two pendulums to kick in and generate club-head speed, there must be consistent hand action. Advanced golfers, who already have consistent hand action, don't need to think about their hands. Everyone else must think about his hands in order to achieve consistent hand action.

For this immensely larger group, all the emphasis on big muscles puts the cart before the horse. The big muscles play a significant role in the golf swing, but it's a supporting role. If the average golfer concentrates on his big muscles as the primary power producer in the golf swing, he forfeits any feel for correct hand action, without which he has no hope of harnessing the potential of centrifugal force.

ACTIVE OR PASSIVE? IT DEPENDS

You hear a lot of talk about "passive" or "active" hands, and I'm not sure the distinction between the two is always clearly drawn. Better players don't want to think about their hands in the golf swing. Learning players need to. That's really the difference between "passive" and "active" hands.

Your hands have to be active when you're learning the game because you may need an early wrist cock to put the shaft in plane when taking the club back and you need to square the club head at impact. Your hands become more passive as you become more established. Active hands play a key role in learning how to draw the ball, passive hands in an antihook swing.

Yes, we want "quiet" hands. But first we must teach them to have sensitivity and feel. Then we quiet them down and make them passive.

In either case, active or passive, your hands must be able to feel the weight of the club head to do their job. That's why "Feel the Club Head" has become a signature mantra of the Nicklaus-Flick Golf School. Your grip pressure needs to be secure enough to keep your club from falling out of control, yet relaxed enough to permit your wrists to cock and uncock naturally in response to centrifugal force.

The right grip pressure allows your hands to become passive on their own. You can't get a death grip on a golf club, then make a conscious decision to "take my hands out of the swing." Rather than *think* your way to passive hands, *train* and *relax* your way there. You don't want to drag or jerk the butt end of the club through impact. You want to allow the club head to release so it can do its job. And that's why you have to—you guessed it—*"Feel the Club Head."*

Quiet hands respond on their own to the weight of the club head. Tight hands have to be told what to do.

○ ○ ○

GOLF IS *NOT* A BIG-MUSCLE GAME

A currently popular school of thought contends that golf is a big-muscle game—and that's partly true for a relative handful of professionals and very low handicappers. For the vast majority of golfers, though, it's just flat wrong. Or, at the very least, dangerously misleading.

Golf, for most golfers, is a small-muscle game in which the big muscles play a supporting role. For the average golfer, focusing on the big muscles to drive the swing is a prescription for frustration. The advanced golfer can learn to use the big muscles correctly and powerfully to support the small muscles. But even then, the big muscles cannot be allowed to *interfere* with the sensitivity and feel of the small muscles

I teach legwork in the golf swing, but I teach it in correct priority and in different manners, depending on my students' abilities, experience, and desired ball flight. For posture, legwork is critical for all students. But for the beginning and intermediate golfer, an active, conscious effort to use the legs during the swing is invariably detrimental.

Today, too many people trying to learn to play golf are being taught to use their legs and hips before they're taught to use their hands and their arms to square the golf club.

> **"First you teach a golfer to hook the ball by using his hands and arms properly. Then you teach him how to take the hook away by using his body and legs properly."**
>
> **—Harvey Penick**

SWINGING ELEMENTS . . .

The effective functioning of the two pendulums—indeed, the very success of the pendulum-like swing—depends on the swinging elements. Indeed, for most golfers, probably 80 percent of your distance comes from the swinging elements. Maybe it's time you got to know them:

1. *The Instrument.* Perhaps that seems too obvious to mention. So how is it that many golfers seem so uncertain about what's happening with the business end of the club in their hands?
2. *The Mind.* You need a concept of how you want to use the instrument—that is, for a pendulum-like swing. You also need an emotional approach that won't get in the way of what you're trying to accomplish by introducing tension.
3. *The Fingers and Hands.* Note that I did not say only hands. Better players control and feel the club with their fingers.
4. *The Wrists.* Your first hinge.
5. *Your Forearms.* They transport the club and keep it on course.
6. *The Elbows.* Your folding units for the backswing and forward swing.
7. *The Upper Arms and Shoulder Sockets.* Your second hinge. The shoulders are *not* used to turning the swing; they are carriers of the swing. The upper arms must be able to move freely under your shoulder sockets.

. . . AND TURNING ELEMENTS

The turning elements are the shoulders, the torso, the hips, the legs, the knees, and the feet. Important? Of course. But they play a subordinate role to the swinging elements.

The turning elements should respond to—and be in harmony with—the swinging elements. The turning elements should *not* control the swinging elements.

Too many people turn first and swing second. That's putting the cart before the horse.

> **"A hit must be perfectly timed, but a swing will time itself."**
>
> —Grantland Rice

GOOD UNDERPINNING

The average player shouldn't be actively thinking about his feet and knees during the swing. In really good players—the tour players I teach, for example—the swinging elements turn the shoulders going back and the feet and legs control the turning elements coming down. I teach a developing player to let his feet and legs support him and move in response to the swing, while I teach a tour-quality player to direct his swing with his feet and legs.

For most golfers, excessive leg motion interferes with the swinging elements. Your body gets moving so much that it's out of harmony with your swing.

As a kid, when you pitched pennies, you would use your legs to support your arm. You wouldn't stand flat-footed and pitch a penny because tension might develop in your arm and your hand would get too tight. You would step with your left leg and swing with your right arm, leaving your wrist and hand to react.

The same thing holds true in chipping and pitching your golf ball. You need your feet and legs for rhythm and support, not for power. So when I teach people about involving their feet and legs in their golf swing, I don't teach them in a full swing. I teach them off the edge of the green so they can feel their feet supporting the motion.

Gentle, natural involvement of the feet and knees—no more than in pitching pennies—allows your arms to stay relaxed while making the chip. If you're going to pitch your ball and your club needs to swing back a little further, then you will have a little more footwork *in response to your longer swing.*

But rather than ask someone to *move* his feet while making part shots, I'll ask him to *feel* his feet moving inside his shoes as he swings the club. There's a difference. And it's the difference between being a mechanical golfer and a feel golfer.

GROUND UP

Jack Nicklaus's longtime teacher, Jack Grout, would have Jack hit balls by the hour without letting either of his heels come off the ground. His ankles could roll back and through, back and through, but Jack couldn't let his back heel come up during his finish. The idea was to develop rhythm from the ground up while not allowing the hips and shoulders to overwork.

Good footwork tends to follow naturally from good posture, good balance, and a relaxed upper body. But I have to be careful introducing footwork to the average golfer because I don't want him standing over the ball thinking about driving his legs. I might say, "Your feet and legs are working well in response to your swing."

○ ○ ○

TENSION PREVENTION

It starts in the mind, goes directly to the hands, the direct contact point with the instrument, then travels up the forearms, settles in the shoulders, and locks you up tighter than a U.S. Open fairway. The only way to stop tension is before it starts.

That sounds like the beginning of some cheesy TV ad, but for athletes, the problems caused by excessive tension are dead serious. Every sports pro I've ever worked with or talked with, from Jimmy Connors to Charles Barkley to Tom Landry, has a battery of techniques and habits to reduce tension.

Anything that creates tension in your mind or body is going to end up hurting your golf game.

The more you try to *hit* rather than *swing*, the more tension will creep into your shoulders and chest and the less freedom you will have in your hands and arms.

SPEED THRILLS

"Slow down your backswing."

How many times has your regular golf partner said that to you?

How many times have you said it to him?

Well, put them together and I'd guess you'd have a pretty big number. Too bad, because the admonition to slow down your backswing, while well intentioned, adds up to a whole lot of off-center hits, at least in the advice department.

The fact is, there is no single, set speed for the backswing that's right for everybody. Watch Nick Price hit his tee shot: he looks as if he's just heard the last call for lunch. Watch Fred Couples and it seems as if he doesn't particularly care if his hands ever make it to the top. Tom Watson is fast. Ernie Els is slow.

The speed of the swing will vary with a golfer's physical and emotional makeup. What's important is not the speed but the *tempo* of the swing.

Still looking for a benchmark? Try this: the start of the pendulum-like swing going away from the ball should *feel like* the first foot or so of the forward swing. Grab a scoring pencil and underline the words "feel like" because I'm not going to come around and put a stopwatch on you.

But if the beginning of your backswing and the beginning of your forward swing feel as if they're in harmony, then chances are pretty good that you've got the right speed for you.

HOW TO DIAL LONG DISTANCE

There are three things that give us distance: club-head speed, center-face hits, and angle of approach. All three have to be present in proper balance.

For instance, a lot of club-head speed isn't going to do much good if you hit the ball on the toe of your club. And if you chop downward with your driver, neither a center-face hit nor lots of club-head speed is going to help. With an iron, on the other hand, you *need* a descending blow to squeeze the ball against the ground and get desired spin and distance.

To get more distance, you *do* need to generate more club-head speed, but please, please, please remember that you can get that with a longer swing, not a harder one. You don't want to monkey around with the law of gravity and centrifugal force.

Relaxed muscles offer the best chance of creating a high level of athletic performance.

THE BLUDGEON

The lightest club in the bag? The driver. That's right. The club you want to hit the farthest is the one you need to hold the lightest and the one with which you need to have your arms the freest. Most people, when they're trying to hit a driver, do the exact opposite.

The idea is to swing the golf club, not hit the ball. A hit requires a sudden application of power. A pendulum-like swing involves a gradual acceleration of power that maxes out at precisely the right time—at impact. Pursuit of a pendulum-like swing puts your mind-set and body in harmony because you're not tensing up to get sudden acceleration.

HORSE BEFORE CART

Am I saying that the golf swing is exclusively the work of your hands and arms? Of course not. *Absolutely not.* For the last several years I have been working closely with Jack Nicklaus. If Jack thought I were advocating a hands-arms-only approach to golf, he'd come after me with a one iron. And everybody knows how well Jack Nicklaus hits his one iron.

What I *am* saying is that the turning elements—the shoulders, the hips, the legs—should respond to the swinging elements—the hands, the wrists, the arms, the instrument. If the turning elements seize control, chances are the proper swing arc will be thrown out of orbit.

Simply put, the swing turns the body both ways, backward and forward. The body does not turn the swing.

If we make a commitment to utilize gravity and centrifugal force in a pendulum-like swing, then we must figure out a way to let the swinging elements do their job.

DRILL: LEFT FOOT, RIGHT TOE

If you have any lingering doubts that the swinging elements are more important in the golf swing than the turning elements, I invite you to try the Left Foot, Right Toe Drill.

Step up to your ball and assume your normal address. Now put all your weight on your left leg and foot, balance on your right toe, and hit some golf balls.

If turning were more important than swinging, and if a conscious weight shift were really the engine of the golf swing, then you'd be in big trouble, wouldn't you? You can't turn your body much if you're standing on one leg, and you can't make a big old weight shift without falling on your butt. By all rights, you shouldn't be able to hit the ball.

But you can.

After a few swings, you find you can hit the ball pretty well. For one thing, it's difficult if not impossible to overswing without losing your balance, so pretty soon you're swinging more rhythmically, more smoothly, just in order to keep from falling down. Your upper body is turning, but only in response to the

Left Foot, Right Toe. This drill proves that 75 to 80 percent of your normal distance comes from the swinging elements, not the turning elements.

swinging of your club. After a while, you're getting about 75 to 80 percent of your normal distance.

In my opinion, in the backswing good players swing first, then they turn. In other words, the swing starts, and as it gets farther back, the body turns in response to and in harmony with all parts of the swing.

So what should the average golfer focus his attention on? The turning elements—the legs, hips, and shoulders—that produce 20 percent of your distance? Or the swinging elements—the hands, wrists, forearms, and elbows—that produce 80 percent of your distance?

Tour players have the 80 percent pretty much knocked—if they didn't, they wouldn't be on the tour—so they mostly concentrate on the 20 percent. Makes sense. And it explains why most of what you read about golf, based as it is on what the tour players do, emphasizes the turning elements.

What doesn't make sense is for golfers who don't have a handle on the 80 percent—and that's about 95 percent of the people who play the game—to become preoccupied with the 20 percent.

The Left Foot, Right Toe Drill helps you play the percentages.

IN BALANCE WITH THE TARGET LINE

The best way to determine whether your club head is swinging in the proper plane is to make sure your club shaft is in balance with the target line—that is, pointing at the target line midway through the backswing and midway through the forward swing.

That would be easy enough to determine with a freeze-frame video of your hands stopped midway between your waist and the top of your backswing. You'd simply draw a straight line extending down from your shaft to the target line.

At midpoint in the backswing, most really good golfers have their shafts pointing inside the target line, or relatively upright. They allow their club head to loop back inside on the forward swing.

Most poor golfers have their shafts pointing outside the target line, or relatively flat. The term for this is "laid off," and while it's not as bad as unemployment, it's close. If your club is laid off, on your forward swing you have to come out and over, your hands get out too far ahead of the club head, and your shoulders or hands have to mount a rescue mission to catch up. Either the shoulders rush forward too fast or the hands flip the club. The usual result? A pull-hook or an ugly slice.

Most golfers who come to the Nicklaus-Flick Golf School don't realize that the same swing—make that the same *flawed* swing—can produce radically different ball flights. That pull-hook and that ugly slice by the same golfer with the same swing on consecutive shots simply means that the rescue mission mounted by the hands and shoulders arrives too soon (the pull-hook) or too late (the ugly slice) to save the swing.

Sometimes, of course, the rescue mission arrives at precisely the correct moment and produces a lovely, perfect, at-long-last-I've-figured-out-this-damned-game shot, smack down the middle of the fairway. That lulls us, for the moment, into believing we finally have a golf swing. Problem is, if our golf swing isn't consistently in harmony with the target line, we won't have it for long.

Now, tell me: wouldn't you rather have your car run consistently and reliably than have to depend on an AAA service truck showing up just in the nick of time so you can get to work

In Balance with Target Line. Midway through the backswing, the club shaft should be pointing directly at the target line.

every day? It's the same with your golf swing. If you depend on a rescue mission from your hands or shoulders to make a good shot, maybe it's time to go shopping for a new swing.

Or at least take the old one in for an overhaul.

The average golfer should try to have his shaft pointing *at* the target line at midpoint in the backswing and again at midpoint in the forward swing. As a general rule, whichever end of the club is closest to the target line should be pointing to the

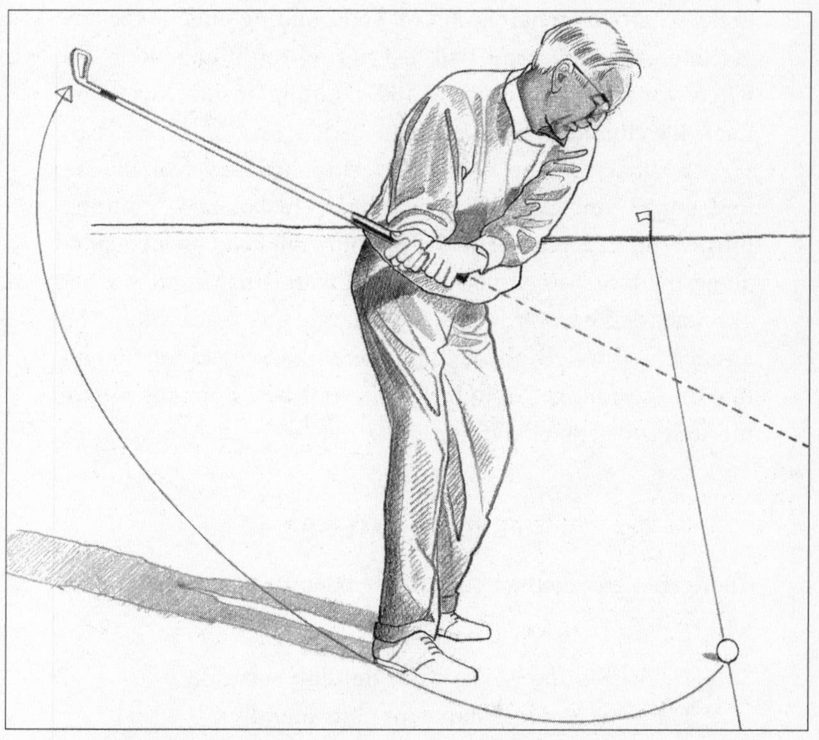

Out of Balance with Target Line. If your club shaft is "laid off" midway through the backswing—that is, pointing outside the target line—a disastrous, over-the-top return to the ball is practically inevitable.

target line or reasonably close to it. I call this keeping the club "in balance" with the target line. It's extremely critical in maintaining the proper swing arc.

Now, is this an absolute? No, but it is a desirable trait to help swings repeat themselves because then you do not have to manipulate the club head to get it on line to strike the ball.

You can't lug video equipment onto the course with you, so how are you going to know when your club is in balance? *By feeling the club head.* With practice and experience, you'll be able to *feel* when your shaft is laid off and pointing outside the target line—the club head will feel heavy. You'll be able to *feel* when your shaft is upright and pointing inside the target line—the club head will feel light.

And what do you *want* your club head to feel like in midswing? You guessed it: *just right*—in balance—pointing toward the target line. This keeps your club head on an inside-along-the-target-line to inside swing path—that is, an arc that approaches the ball from inside the target line, tracks along the target line through impact, and comes back inside the target line during follow-through. This is your best hope for square hits and consistent ball flight.

FEEL THE MUSIC

There are three distinct but complementary movements in the golf swing:

1. The hands and wrists move the club vertically.
2. The arms and legs move the club laterally.
3. The shoulders and hips impart a rotary movement.

With so many things going on at the same time, there's a lot of potential for mishap unless the three movements occur in harmony. They need to be blended to make sure that your club head stays in an arc that's in balance with the target line. The shorter the club, the closer you stand to the ball and the more vertical the arc will be. With your driver, your club will be in a relatively flatter plane.

You obviously can't see where your club head is at all times during the swing, not unless you have eyes in the back of your head and/or plan to swing your club in extreme slo-mo. So how are you going to know whether it's in the right arc?

By feel.

From a good setup, swing your club back just past waist-high, to a point midway between your shoulders and your waist. Where's your club head? Don't look! Feel it! Feel it with the two middle fingers of your right hand. If you feel pressure on those two fingers, it means your club is laid off, your shaft is out of balance with the target line, and you're in perfect position to launch an over-the-top lunge.

Now, if you can feel that, you have something to work on. But first you have to feel it, and feeling has to be developed and nurtured with a lot of swings on the Training Ground.

I have never known a good player who couldn't tell you exactly where his club head was and what it was doing. Like any good craftsman, a good golfer develops sensitivity for his instrument. And he doesn't do it by worrying exclusively (or even primarily) about weight shift and mechanics. If you're preoccupied with what your shoulders and hips are doing, then you will lose feel for what your instrument is doing.

Is there more to the golf swing? Of course. But it starts with "feeling the club head." That's why better golfers who are having trouble with their full-swing shots almost always go back to their short game for help. That's where they first experienced "feel" in golf, and that's where they return to recover it.

Ever had a great dance partner? Two bodies moving in harmony without conscious direction because they feel the music together? Well, keeping your club head in an arc that's in balance with the target line may not exactly be Fred and Ginger, but to tell you the truth, I'd rather play golf than dance.

SCORECARD SUMMARY

- Pendulum-like swing utilizes gravity and centrifugal force.
- Pendulum-like swing generates maximum club-head speed at bottom of the arc, which is more likely to produce center club-face hits and is more likely to repeat.
- Excessive effort creates excessive tension.
- Small muscles must be trained before big muscles.
- Swinging elements provide 80 percent of the distance generated by the golf swing.
- Turning elements play a subordinate role to swinging elements.
- Anything that creates tension is going to hurt your golf game.
- Key Concept: *Keep shaft of club in balance with target line.*

LESSON 6

THE SWING'S THE THING

ONE OF THE COMFORTING things about golf is that it never really changes. In other sports, techniques change constantly—does anyone even *remember* basketball's two-handed set shot?—but in golf, the mechanics are essentially constant. Sure, Tiger Woods hits the ball farther than anyone in Jack Nicklaus's heyday, just as Jack hit the ball a lot longer than anyone from the Hogan era. But can Tiger Woods learn from studying Hogan's and Nicklaus's swings? You bet. The essence of the basic golf swing hasn't changed much at all, except in response to changes in equipment. All that's changed are the various ways we try to *teach* that swing.

But while there is a timeless consistency to golf for everyone and anyone, there is also a great dichotomy that all golfers must deal with: golf is really two different games. There's the game the pros and better amateurs play, and there's the game everybody else plays.

On the surface, they may look the same, but they're not. I can't teach you to play like Tiger Woods or Jack Nicklaus or Ben Hogan. No teacher can. I can't guarantee to lower your score by a certain number of strokes. No teacher should.

What I *can* do is teach you some basic principles about mental approach and swing mechanics that will allow you to *improve* your score, gain greater consistency, and—I trust—get more fun out of playing the game.

Want an example of what I mean about the two different games of golf? Consider the career of Ben Hogan, who became the best player of his time by eliminating his duck hook. How did he do that? First he developed a weak grip, which is an antihook grip. But the average golfer is constantly fighting a slice, so he needs exactly the opposite approach—he needs a strong grip, which is an antislice grip.

Then Hogan restricted his backswing, taking away a lot of superfluous motion. But most golfers don't have enough backswing to begin with.

Next Hogan drove his body forward and around with his legs to inhibit the club face from turning over and down the way it did with his old hook swing. He activated his legs and hips on the forward swing for more efficiency—and he was able to do it without interrupting the flow of his swing because of years of practice at putting the club face on the ball.

The average golfer, when he tries to "drive" his hips, fractures the rhythm and balance of his swing. He'll be lucky to find the ball with his club head at all. He certainly won't be able to produce square hits consistently.

The issue here is that most *good* golfers, at one time or another, have had to fight a tendency to hook, while most other folks—say, 85 to 90 percent of the people who play the game—spend their time in frustration, fighting a tendency to slice.

Hogan fixed exactly what he had to fix to get rid of his persistent hook, and that was the key to his becoming a better player. But one man's dessert is another man's poison. What worked for Ben Hogan will probably not work for the average golfer.

Unfortunately for the average golfer, much modern teaching of the golf swing derives from a mechanical interpretation of the technical adjustments Ben Hogan made in his own swing and later wrote about in *Five Lessons*. Make that a *partial* interpretation because today's advocates of the big-muscle game and the One-Piece Takeaway neglected the *soul* that was at the heart of Ben Hogan's game. He was *not,* his on-course demeanor and his absorption in technique notwithstanding, a mechanical player. He was a *feel* player with a brilliant understanding of swing mechanics.

For perhaps as many as nine out of ten golfers today, the antihook measures that Hogan took to fix his own swing and that subsequent interpreters have elaborated into a mechanical, big-muscle philosophy are just flat-out the wrong prescription. Good medicine, wrong malady.

Better medicine is a pendulum-like swing based on correct usage of the body's swinging elements.

In studying the swings of the game's best players, I've concluded they have three common traits:

1. **The hands and the club shaft return to the starting position at impact.**
2. **The head returns to its starting position or moves slightly to the golfer's right at impact.**
3. **The left knee and foot—*not* the hips or shoulders—control the change of direction.**

TWO SWINGS

For most golfers, I prescribe what I call the Developmental Swing, which is essentially an *antislice* swing. It calls for early wrist action, an inside-out swing path with the club face rotating down and over, and a high finish. This creates a closing club face at impact, which in turn produces a draw. There is *no* conscious effort to kick out the left knee or turn the hips.

For the tour players and better amateurs I work with, I teach what I call the Professional Swing, which is essentially an *antihook* swing. The Professional Swing calls for more active involvement of the legs and thighs in initiating the forward swing. There is minimal rotation of the club face during the swing, especially in the impact area. The path taken by the club head on the forward swing is inside-along-the-target-line back to inside. The player using the Professional Swing feels as if the club face is staying open longer through impact and working under and up. The finish is more around the body than high.

When the golfer who starts with the Developmental Swing gets to the point at which he can consistently draw the ball, I begin to introduce aspects of the Professional Swing. What that involves is changing the swing path from inside out to more down the target line and back inside after impact, with the club head feeling more open.

You have to understand that one swing is set up to draw the ball, the other to eliminate the possibility of a hook or pull and introduce a fade, so the worst thing you can do is mix and match them.

Unfortunately, that's *exactly* what many golfers do. They'll read how one pro does something here, how another does something there, add a third thing told them by a friend who has a brother-in-law who once was standing next to somebody who got Arnold Palmer's autograph. Pretty soon they have a golf swing that looks as if it was put together from spare parts picked up at a garage sale.

Here are the basic elements that distinguish the two swings:

THE DEVELOPMENTAL SWING

1. Shoulders and hips square to slightly closed at address.
2. Early wrist cock.
3. Swing arc in to out through impact.
4. Club face rotates and turns down through impact.
5. Legs and hips respond to swing motion.
6. Ball flight: right to left.
7. Finish with arms high.

THE PROFESSIONAL SWING

1. Shoulders and hips fractionally open at address.
2. Passive wrists.
3. Swing arc inside-along-the-target-line inside through impact.
4. Club face square through impact.
5. Forward swing initiated by left foot and left knee.
6. Ball flight: straight or left to right.
7. Finish with arms around the body.

The first order of business in the Developmental Swing is to train the swinging elements—the small muscles—so they can find the ball. Then you have to make sure that the turning elements—the big muscles—operate in harmony and support.

The turning elements are used to support—as in "give assistance to," not "be in control of"—the swinging elements. The turning elements are *not* used for power; they help provide rhythm, balance, and timing.

You don't hear much about the swinging elements from tour pros, and for good reason: if they hadn't already mastered the use of the swinging elements, they wouldn't be on the tour. Yet so much of what is written today about the golf swing is based on what the tour players are trying to do and on what great teachers are teaching their tour players—and that's exactly opposite what the average person needs to learn about.

To repeat: *most* golfers need to stick with the Developmental Swing until they learn to use their hands properly to generate distance and to draw the ball.

The Developmental Swing has its limitations, mainly because it requires relatively active hands, which in turn require careful timing. Also, as you get better at delivering the club head from the inside on the forward swing, the Developmental Swing can produce a hook problem. That's when I would begin to introduce elements of the Professional Swing, in which the hands become less active through the impact area.

GET A GRIP

The golf swing begins with a good grip. Without one, you don't have a prayer of developing a consistent game. With one, you solve a lot of swing problems before you even take back your club. No fundamental is more influential than a good grip in helping the club face arrive consistently and squarely at the point of impact.

Here are the seven steps to a good grip:

1. Let your left arm hang down to your side and roll your fingers upward and inward.
2. Place the butt end of the club against the pad of flesh at the heel of your left hand below your middle finger—*not* in your palm.
3. Grasp the club with your fingers and roll your left thumb over the top of your club so that the V formed by your thumb and first finger points at your right shoulder. You should be able to see the first three knuckles of your left hand. This is an antislice, or "strong," grip.

4. Place the fingers of your right hand on the club snugly next to your left hand.
5. Anchor the little finger of your right hand between the first two fingers of your left hand. This is the overlapping grip and should be used by most golfers.
6. The club should be held along the middle joints of the middle two fingers of your right hand. Most nonprofessional golfers I see—maybe 90 percent—hold the club too much in their palms. If you are to have feel in your golf swing, it must begin in your fingers.
7. Fold the thumb of your right hand over the thumb of your left hand. You should have a snug fit, with the V formed by pressing your right thumb against the base of your right finger pointing to your right shoulder. The first finger of your right hand should extend slightly down the club as if it were grasping a trigger. This completes the antislice grip.

To be able to make maximum use of centrifugal force and to insure a free, unfettered swing, hold the club in your fingers, not your palms. This is especially important for beginning and intermediate players who are still developing feel and sensitivity for their instrument. Advanced players may have the club a little more in the palm of their left hand, but that's an antihook grip.

Make sure your hands fit snugly together on the club, but don't jam them hard together—that will introduce tension. You want them to function in harmony throughout the swing, so you can't afford any gaps or air pockets that might contribute to breakdown. You wouldn't move your furniture cross-country in the back of a moving van if it were thrown in there loose, would you? If your hands come apart at the top of the backswing, it will be well-nigh impossible to keep the club on a plane and under control during the forward swing.

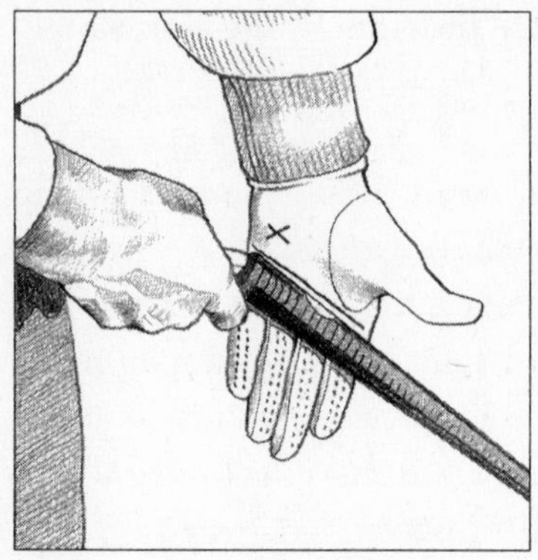

The Grip: Starting Lineup. With your left hand open, place the butt end of the shaft along the line where the fingers join the hand.

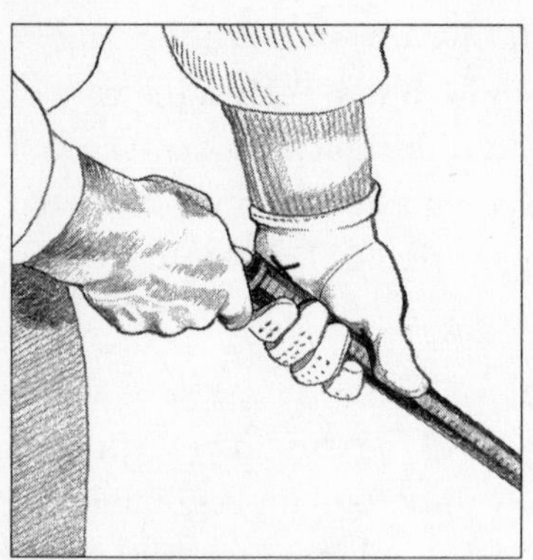

The Grip: X Marks the Spot. The butt end of the shaft fits against the pad of flesh at the heel of your left hand, *not* down in your palm.

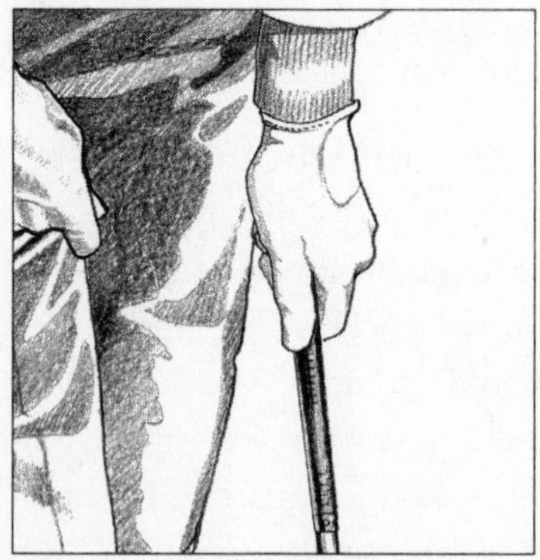

The Grip: Count Your Knuckles. Grasp the club with your fingers and roll your left thumb over the top of the shaft. For an anti-slice or "strong" grip, you should be able to see the first three knuckles of your left hand, with the V formed by your left thumb and first finger pointing to your right shoulder.

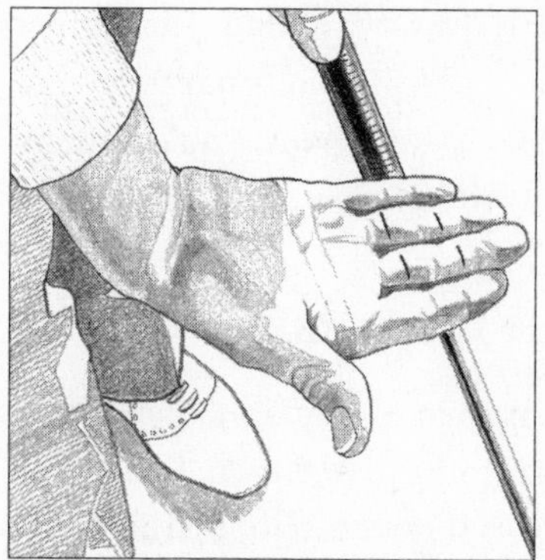

The Grip: Where Feel Begins. Hold your club against the middle two fingers of your right hand. *Do not* grab it down in your palm.

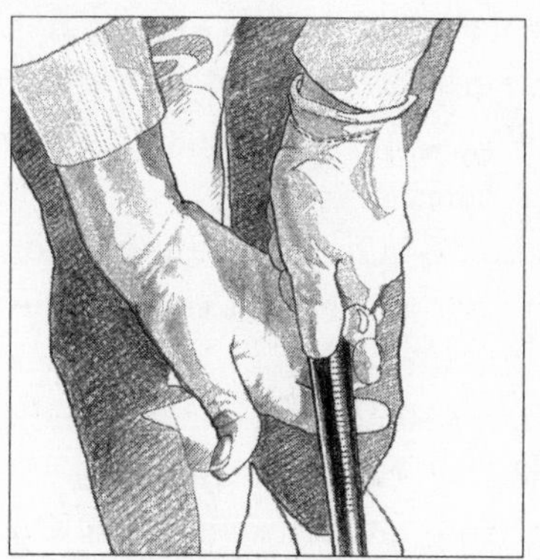

The Grip: Overlap to Anchor. Secure the little finger of your right hand between the first two fingers of your left hand. This overlapping grip should be used by most golfers.

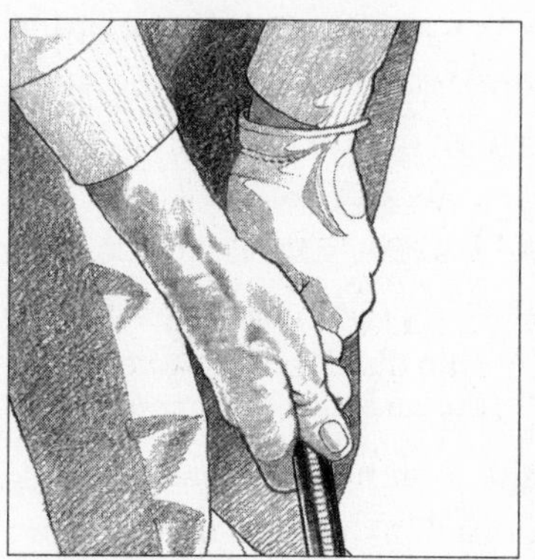

The Grip: Finishing Touch. Fold the right thumb over the top of your left thumb. Think snug, not tight. The V formed by pressing your right thumb against the base of your right finger should point to your right shoulder.

Please note that I said "snugly," not "tightly." The tighter your grip is, the less you'll be able to feel what's happening to your club head during the swing. And I think you know by now how much importance I attach to feel.

DON'T CRUSH THAT BIRD

You have a bird in the hand . . . ah, hands. You don't want to let the bird go, but you don't want to hurt it, either. *That's* how you want to grip your golf club: as if it were a living thing that you want to hold without hurting.

Since you probably don't have any spare birds in your golf bag with which to practice your grip pressure, it seems to me you need another test—one you can take regularly. Well, you're in luck. I've got one right here.

Take your regular grip and hold your club out in front of you, parallel to the ground. Have a friend take the club head in his hands and twist it. If the club turns in your hands, your grip is too loose. If he encounters resistance in turning the club, your grip is too tight. Just right? That's when the club stays securely in your hands but your hands and arms react easily to his twisting of the club head.

Correct grip pressure allows the weight in the head of the golf club to utilize centrifugal force and gravity. It's critical that you feel the weight and the position of the club head through the entire golf swing. Obviously you can't do that if you have a death grip on the butt end. Nor, for that matter, can you do it if your grip's so loose that the club wobbles in your hands.

All the ball knows is what the club head tells it, so it stands to reason that you want a grip that lets you sense where the club head is at all times. Note that I said "sense" and not "understand." Understanding requires thinking, and the last thing in the world you want to be doing in the middle of your golf swing is trying to control it with conscious mental direction.

I cannot emphasize enough the importance of secure but light grip pressure in the golf swing. If you grip the club too tightly, you introduce tension into your forearms, and tension will sabotage your swing before you even take the club back. If you gain nothing else from this book, I hope you come away with respect and appreciation for correct grip pressure.

FLOAT LIKE A BUTTERFLY

Just because you want to position your club head square to the target line behind your ball doesn't mean you want it to sit there.

If you rest your club head on the ground behind your ball, you'll have to lift or pull it off the ground when you start your backswing. And when you do, your grip pressure will almost certainly change, if only fractionally.

Once you've squared your club head to the target line in your Pre-Shot Routine, hover it behind the ball, just brushing the grass, in the second or so before you begin your backswing. That way you can take the club back without any change in grip pressure.

POSTURE

Next to correct grip pressure, nothing is more critical to the success of your golf swing than correct posture. It's your posture that gives your arms room to swing. Here is the sequence of steps to perfect golf posture for full-swing shots:

1. Stand tall, shoulders back, head up, just like your mother told you to. Not rigid, mind you: this isn't the army, and nobody yelled, "Ten-hut!"
2. Bend forward at the hips *first,* keeping your back "tall" and chin up off your chest. You want your arms to be able to swing underneath your shoulder sockets, and your shoulders to be able to pass under your chin.
3. Flex your knees *slightly*—about three to four inches—while allowing your weight to go to the balls of your feet. This is superimportant: the deeper your knee flex, the more your weight goes back on your heels, causing your back to tilt up to vertical. When your back gets too vertical, your arms have to swing around on too flat a plane, resulting in your club being laid off. When your club is laid off—that is, when the shaft midway between the waist and the top of the backswing is pointing outside the target line rather than at or inside it—an over-the-top forward swing is inevitable. And when *that* happens, it's usually "Fore, *left!*" or "Fore, *right!*"—almost never "Golf shot!"
4. Tilt your torso *slightly* to the right so that when your right hand slides under your left on the club, your right shoulder is slightly lower than the left. You want your spine angle tilted from the top to the base of your spine with your belly button fractionally closer to the target than your throat. This helps you swing from the inside.

If you've been playing with bad posture—too much knee flex, back bowed, chin on chest, weight on heels, any or all of these—then your new posture is going to feel strange for a while. You won't like it. You'll feel as if you're going to pitch forward. That's why you need to practice this away from the golf course until it feels absolutely comfortable.

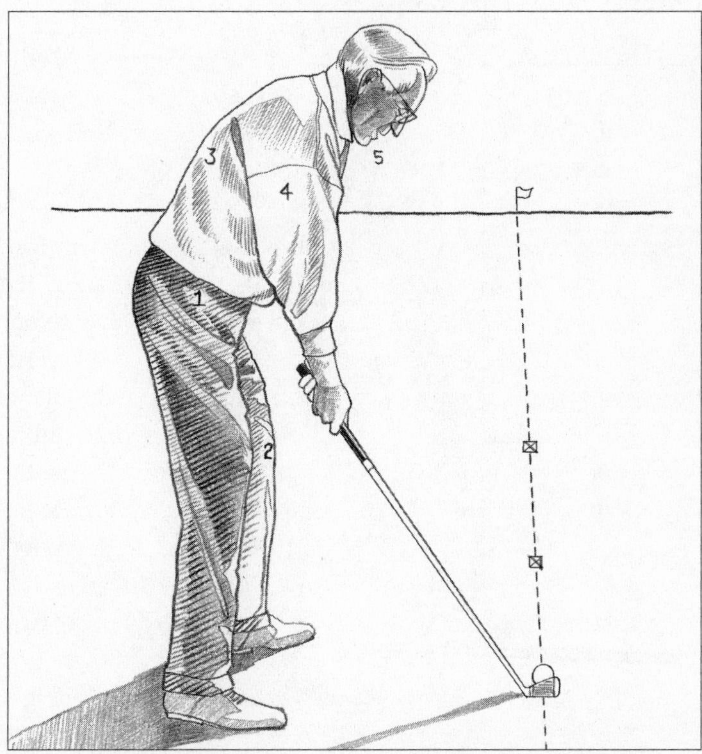

Get Set. First, to establish your target line, place your club so that the face is square to the target line, and fit your body to the club. Then (1) bend forward at the hips, (2) flex your knees slightly, (3) keep your back straight, (4) be in a position that lets your arms hang freely from your shoulder sockets, and (5) keep your chin up.

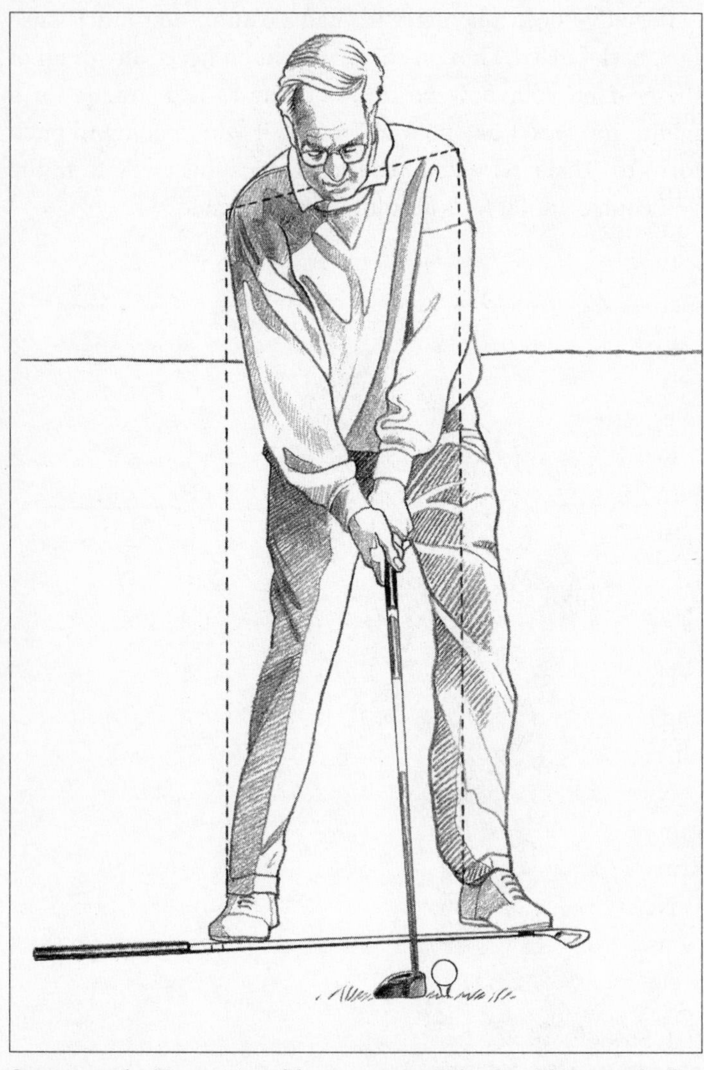

Square to the Target. At address, your weight should be evenly distributed between both legs. Because your right hand is below your left hand on the club shaft, your right shoulder will necessarily be slightly lower than your left—about this much with a wood, a bit more so with an iron because of the shorter shaft.

KNEE FLEX TEST

Limiting your knee flex is crucial. The deeper your knee flexes, the more your quadriceps muscles tense up, and tense quads restrict hip rotation. When you're standing tall, bending at the hips, your hips can respond more easily to the swinging of your arms. Here's a quick way to test your knee flex:

With knees flexed at what you feel is the proper amount, place a golf club across your kneecaps. Now, while holding the club in place in front of your knees, lock your knees. The space between the shaft of your club and your knees should be between three and four inches.

Remember: the concept is to make the swinging of the arms turn the body. That can't happen if your body's not in the right position.

DRILL: "FEEL THE CLUB HEAD"

Hold your club straight up, perpendicular to the ground, and feel the weight of the club head. Can't feel the club head at all, right? Too light.

Now hold it straight out in front of you, parallel to the ground. Causes a little pull at the top of your wrists and forearms, right? Too heavy.

Now hold it pointing halfway between the first two positions. Close your eyes. Focus on the weight you feel. That's the weight you want to feel throughout your golf swing. Just right.

1. Straight up, too light.
2. Straight out, too heavy.
3. In between, just right.

○ ○ ○

Just Right. Straight up, the club head is too light to feel. Straight out, it's too heavy. Halfway between, ahhh . . .

POSTURE, GRIP PRESSURE—AND SWING ARC

Three interrelated factors contribute to make the two pendulums work in harmony.

One is the aim of your club and your posture. If your posture's not right, then you can't keep the club swinging in the right arc.

The second factor is a constant light grip pressure that allows centrifugal force to generate club-head speed.

The third is a swing arc that does not require a lot of manipulation of the club face.

The backswing and the forward swing must move in the correct arc, with the forward swing matching the backswing so that the club can be in a balanced position to find the golf ball. If they're not in the correct arc, then you've got to compensate by manipulating the shaft and club face to square the club face at impact. And that just isn't going to work consistently.

TAKE THE DIRECT ROUTE

If you were driving from California to Georgia and took a left turn at Louisiana, you'd probably miss your tee time at Augusta National, wouldn't you? By the same token, if your arms and club pick the wrong route on the backswing and forward swing, your club head is going to have a hard time getting to its intended designation. Makes sense, doesn't it?

Consider, for instance, what happens when your hands run out and away from your legs on the backswing. Either your hands start twisting or your shoulders start turning—or both—and your club shaft gets laid off behind you. From that position, the only place your arms and club have to go on the forward swing is over the top on an outside-in path to your ball. The result is ugly.

The solution, though, is not to work on turning your torso more. The solution is to work on getting your arms in the correct routing so that their movement turns the torso, first back, then forward.

Arnold Palmer used to say that if the first foot of the backswing is correct, the rest of the swing will take care of itself. I'd like to amend that to three feet and state it this way: if you keep your club head in front of your hands until they are about waist-high on your backswing, you're on the right road for your round-trip back to your ball.

Try this: on your backswing, make the little finger on your left hand feel as if it's going to brush your right pants leg. In other words, don't let the space between your hands and your legs increase during the backswing. Taking this path will help you stand the club head up along the right arc, and it will turn your upper torso for you.

If you want to be sure of getting to the right place at the right time, take the direct route.

ROUND-TRIP TICKET

Study the swings of golf's greatest players—and I have—and you discover one thing they have in common: on the forward swing, they return their clubs to the shaft plane line of the starting position.

Do a freeze-frame at impact. The chin is behind the ball. The hands are back at the starting position. The club shaft looks to be in exactly the same place it started. Depending on the golfer, you'll see differences in where various body parts are (legs, knees, shoulders), but the chin, the hands, and the shaft are in virtually identical positions.

They achieved this not by thinking about shifting their weight but by applying the club head to the ball. That's Jack Nicklaus's term—"applying the club head to the ball"—and I love it.

If you're trying to clear your hips, you very likely won't leave enough room for your hands and arms to get the club head back down to the starting position. As Stan Thirsk, Tom

Watson's teacher, puts it, "Your body must not invade the space your arms need."

Why set up a roadblock when you don't have to?

HE'S GOT RHYTHM

Ernie Els, the 1994 U.S. Open champion from South Africa, ranks right up there with Tiger Woods and Phil Mickelson on my short list of the best young golfers in the game today. He has a sweeping, classical swing that reminds me of Sam Snead's. Much more powerfully built than Sam, Ernie looks as if he could hit the ball a mile. And he can.

But Els doesn't get his distance just—or even primarily—from his physical strength. Like Sam, he has marvelous rhythm and balance.

I asked Ernie once how he came by his great rhythm. He said that when he first started playing golf, his mother gave him one of those practice balls that won't go more than about forty yards no matter how hard you hit it. A big, strapping kid, Ernie said he would take the ball out into his front yard and swing as hard as he could. The result: forty yards. After a while, he'd swing easy. The result: forty yards. When he got to the golf course, he found that his easier, more rhythmical swings hit the ball *farther* than his hard swings.

So when you watch that graceful, fluid swing of Ernie Els, give some credit to his mom.

SPINE ANGLE

A basic move in the macarena?

The name of the rock-and-roll group that opens for Spinal Tap?

A breakthrough concept in the new field of biogeometrics?

Could be all of them for all I know.

What I *do* know for sure is that "spine angle" is a critically important golf term referring to the angle formed by the spine and the legs at address.

Maintaining your spine angle throughout the swing is a key element in consistency. If your spine angle changes during your swing—that is, if you lift your body—the freedom of your wrist hinge is compromised and your hands have to get overly active to square the club face at impact. The frequent result: a big slice or a pull-hook, caused by "coming out" of your swing.

You can forget everything else you were taught about geometry, but whatever you do, *don't* forget about spine angle.

HOW WIDE?

The width of your stance will vary according to the shot to be played. For full-swing iron shots, your feet should be approximately shoulder-width apart. For shots off a tee, perhaps a little wider. For chips and pitches, bring your feet closer together. Taller golfers will feel more stable with a marginally wider stance.

FANCY FOOTWORK

Ever notice how Ray Floyd shuffles his feet while he's waggling his club at address? It's not because Raymond has a bad case of athlete's foot or is scared he might whiff or needs to visit the Port-O-San. It's because he understands the important but subtle role the feet play in the golf swing.

That little foot shuffle is part of Floyd's Pre-Shot Routine because he's setting himself physically to *feel* what he's about to

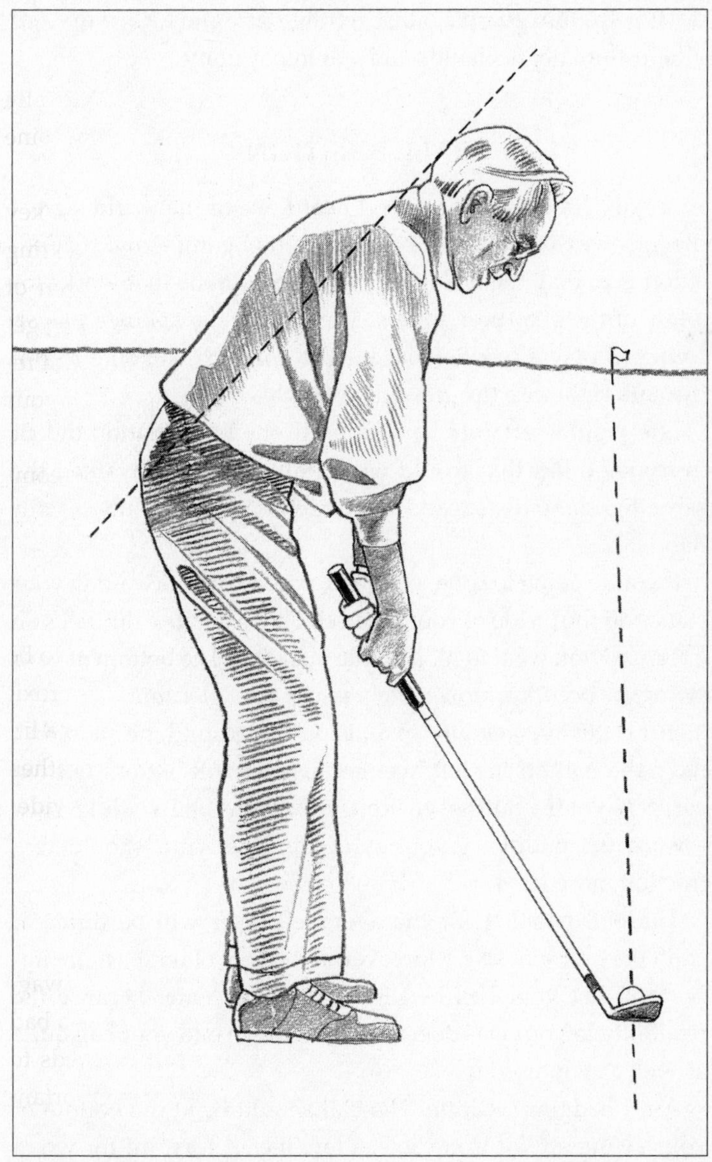

Spine Angle. You won't find anything about it in Euclid, but this is the most important angle in golf.

do. It helps him guard against getting static and locked up, and it helps him get his hands and feet in harmony.

BALL POSITION

At a golf clinic overseas once, I heard one of the world's great players say that golf is a one-ball-position game—and that position is to play the ball off the left heel. Maybe that works for a few of the very best golfers. Maybe. But the average player, trying to play a wedge with his ball forward, is going to run the club right into the ground behind his ball.

Life would certainly be simpler if one ball position did fit every shot. But that would work only if you always had the same lie, same distance to the target, and same club in your hands.

If you're going to drive your ball, you want it forward in your stance off the inside of your left heel. That's because the ball's on a tee, and you want to hit it on the upswing. The bottom of your swing arc occurs approximately under your sternum.

But if the average guy's ball is on the ground, he shouldn't have the ball off his left heel because he will bottom out too early. If you're hitting an iron, move the ball slightly back toward the middle of your stance and get your shoulders a fraction more level.

The ball position for the average player will be different from the tour player's. Moreover, as you get older it's more important that your ball be slightly toward center because the flexibility in your legs doesn't let you move into your ball quite as well as you used to.

Am I hedging? A little. The ball should be at the bottom of your swing arc for iron shots, a few inches forward for wood shots off a tee. But the bottom of the swing arc is going to vary slightly, depending on your height, shape of swing, flexibility, and use of your body. So I prefer to think of a ball position *zone* that, for full-swing shots, ranges from dead center to the inside of the left heel.

For most golfers, the rule of thumb for full-swing shots is as follows: with a wood, play any ball on a tee inside your left heel; with an iron, play any ball on the ground toward the center of your stance. The exact location will vary according to the length of the club, with the ball at the center of your stance for short-iron shots and fractionally forward for mid- and long-iron shots. As in every part of the game, trial and error is necessary to find what position suits *your* swing best.

FOUR REASONS WHY A SWING WORKS BETTER THAN A HIT

1. With a swing, you're more likely to create maximum clubhead speed at the appropriate time, which is at the bottom of the arc.
2. With a swing, you're less likely to twist the club face in an effort to create more speed.
3. With a swing, you're more likely to hit the ball in the center of the club face.
4. With a swing, you enlist centrifugal force and gravity as allies in your quest for consistency.

WHY YOU SHOULD BECOME A HAPPY HOOKER

"You can talk to a slice," Lee Trevino is fond of saying, "but you can't talk to a hook." It's sure worked for him. Nobody speaks the language of the left-to-right world better than Lee Trevino.

But what about the guy who hopes to go from a twenty handicap to a fourteen, or even from a sixteen to a ten? The best thing for him to do is to learn to draw the ball.

Let's be realistic: it's pointless for golfers with double-digit handicaps to think about "working the ball." You have to be honest with yourself. Are you going to be able to work the ball left or right when you play twenty to twenty-five times a year or even once a week? No. You want to hit it far, and you want to play the game. The best way to do that is to learn to draw the ball.

Think of learning to move the ball right to left as a step toward greatness. After all, there's never been a great golfer who didn't go through a period of having to fight a hook.

If you reach a certain skill level and have a certain commitment level, then perhaps the fade is the shot for you. But until then, stick with learning to draw the ball.

THE PROBLEM WITH YOUR DRIVER

"Except for the driver, every club has its distance limitations," a student told me recently. "The driver has unlimited potential—and that's what gets me in trouble."

He's right. When you pick up a six iron, you know just about how far it's going to go. And if it's not quite enough, you don't try to hit it harder—you pull out a five iron.

But people have a tendency to see the driver—subconsciously, at least—as having no distance limitations. That sometimes encourages a wild, out-of-control power surge that generally results in a mis-hit.

Anyone with a handicap above fifteen to eighteen should, in my opinion, keep his driver in his car trunk and use a three wood off the tee. Not just because a driver's harder to hit and the extra fifteen yards or so isn't worth the sacrifice in accuracy, but also because it keeps a golfer from getting seduced by his driver's "unlimited" potential.

"DON'T SHIFT YOUR WEIGHT!"

I thought that might get your attention.

Please note that I did *not* say, "Your weight doesn't shift"—obviously, it does. With a natural, free, in-balance swing, it has to. My point is that you don't have to make a conscious effort to shift your weight; with a correct setup and aim, your effort to swing your club will shift it.

A mechanical approach to creating a pivot or a weight shift turns an effect into a cause, i.e., makes turning the shoulders and driving the hips the *cause* of the club moving. Those things should be the *result* of the club moving.

Ninety percent of teaching today emphasizes the idea of the body moving the club rather than the body moving in response to the use of the club. This is an important—a critical—distinction to understand if your golf game is to be based on feel and sensitivity.

Jack Grout taught Jack Nicklaus to get a bigger, longer (and consequently more powerful) motion by swinging his club to the sky. He didn't tell him to shift his weight on the forward swing. He told him to apply the club head to the ball—and that's what shifted the weight.

The body moves because of what you're doing with the club. A weight shift is the effect of your use of the club. A conscious effort to shift your weight is antithetical to rhythm. It's a mechanical response that destroys feel and makes the golf swing hard to time and repeat.

If you practice a mechanical weight shift, you will make your body dominate and take over from the free swinging of the arms. Can some players consciously shift their weight and still make their club find the ball? Certainly: pros and low-single-digit handicappers can. What about the average golfer? No way, at least not consistently.

Learning how to use your club is the big deal: you should build your approach to the game around what your club is doing. When I open a session of the Nicklaus-Flick Golf School, one of the first things I do is have students watch an instructor hit a few balls. Then I ask them to tell me *exactly* what they were watching. You'd be amazed at how many watch the instructor's body and how many watch the ball—and how few watch the club. Well, guess what? It's the club that actually hits the ball. It's the club that makes the ball go to the target. So let the use of your club tell your body what to do, not vice versa. Without harmony between body and club, your golf game can have no soul.

The game of golf is not about what your body is doing. It's about what your club head is doing as it delivers its message to the ball.

THE HOME STRETCH

The body needs to be flexible so it can turn in response to the movement of the club head. That's why we do stretching exercises at the Nicklaus-Flick Golf School. That's why you should do stretching exercises before going onto the golf course or the practice range.

A few years ago the PGA measured the shoulder turn (with a driver) of the thirty leading money winners. The minimum: 93 degrees. The maximum: *110* degrees. Can the average guy turn that far without completely destroying the rhythm of his swing? Almost certainly not. That's one of the big reasons it's pointless trying to get someone to work on turning his body at the expense of feeling his golf club.

Sometimes I do have to get a golfer to think consciously about his turn, but only when his body type or restricted flexibility does not permit adequate turn in natural response to the swinging of the club. Even then, conscious thinking about a shoulder turn is not something I would ever prescribe for an extended period of time because of its potentially unpleasant side effects.

The good news? You can do something fairly simple and easy to improve your flexibility. That's why I devote a whole chapter to exercises that you can do at home.

DON'T CARRY THE TRAY

Some people advocate the "tray position" at the top of the swing, with the right wrist bent as if you were carrying a tray. I think the tray position is dead wrong because it causes the club face to become too closed.

I want to see your right wrist more *under* the shaft at the top, not bent backward. From this position, you'll be more able to deliver the club downward from the inside in the correct routing on the forward swing.

○ ○ ○

LET THE AIR OUT

The change of direction—that is, the point at which the backswing ends and the forward swing begins—is where you need to blend the swinging elements and the turning elements. If you don't have proper support from the feet and legs, then your swing will be threatened by overactivity of the shoulders and torso in the change of direction.

The change of direction must *not* be initiated by the shoulders—it's critical that your arms remain relaxed. If you are consciously trying to shift your weight by driving this or that part of your body, there is an implicit urgency, an ever-present threat of destructive abruptness. This creates tension, the worst possible condition that can creep into a golf swing. If your swing is built on the pendulum concept, there should no urgency at the top of your swing, no abruptness at the change of direction.

Many tour players will tell you they want to soften their arms precisely at the change of direction. I think that's one thing the pros do that is 100 percent applicable to *all* golfers. With your shoulders still fully turned, you want to feel as if your arms just drop in response to the pull of gravity. From the top of the swing, it's the same move you'd make if you were putting your right hand in your right hip pocket.

The last thing you want to be thinking at this critical point in the golf swing is "hit," much less "kill it." Either thought will almost invariably produce tighter grip pressure, an abrupt forward lurch of the shoulders, increased tension—and a rushed, arrhythmic, out-of-control slash.

Save that one for the next time you're attacked by a sabertoothed tiger.

The operative image at the change of direction in the golf swing should be, in the words of sports kinesiologist Gideon Ariel, "Let the air out of my arms."

> **"If I put the club in the right position at the top of my backswing, I'll be turned properly. And if I apply the club head to the ball correctly, my weight will shift."**
>
> —Jack Nicklaus

RUNAWAY–CATCH UP

Never heard of Runaway–Catch Up? Sounds like an old-fashioned kids' game, but in fact it's one of the most common problems in golf. It begins at the change of direction, that point in the golf swing when the backswing ends and the forward swing commences.

There's no question that the change of direction of the golf swing starts with the left heel going down and the left knee moving laterally. But in trying consciously to make their swing work that way, most folks don't get their backswing completed, and their body—particularly their hips—runs out ahead of their hands. That leads to Runaway–Catch Up.

What happens is as simple as it is devastating: the body runs away, opens toward the target too fast, and the hands are forced to play catch-up. Instead of dropping the club along the same arc or slightly inside of the backswing, the arms and hands are jerked by the movement of the shoulders and hips. The club head goes out of plane and over the top. From this point, all hope of a good swing is lost.

Oh, you'll hit a good shot now and then because the last-instant manipulating of the club will occasionally square up the club face at impact with the ball. Most of the time, though, Runaway–Catch Up is a no-win game.

HANG TIME

If your posture doesn't allow your arms to hang freely from your shoulder sockets, then they can't swing freely. And if your arms can't swing freely, tension will destroy your rhythm, your balance, and—ultimately—your chances of making a consistent golf swing.

POWER CORRUPTS

The pursuit of power is one of the most dangerous things in golf. It leads to overactive legs and an overactive body, it introduces tension into the golf swing, it undermines feel for the club, and it gives disproportionate emphasis to just one aspect of the game. About the only positive contribution of uncontrolled pursuit of power is to make golf ball and equipment manufacturers rich.

Look at what it's done to so many players on the PGA Tour. Ian Baker-Finch, who won the 1991 British Open, decided he wanted to hit his ball farther. So he changed his swing—and stopped making cuts, much less winning tournaments. Kenny Knox played with John Daly in the last round at Crooked Stick when Daly came out of nowhere to win the 1991 PGA. Knox was a good, solid player whose career seemed on the rise, but he got so spooked by being outdriven seventy-five yards by Daly that he gave his swing a complete overhaul, looking for more power. Has anybody seen Kenny Knox on a leader board since?

What happens to so many players—beginning, average, and good players alike—is that the pursuit of hitting their ball farther gets them out of what they can realistically repeat. What most golfers don't understand is that when you're pursuing more distance, you must think in terms of increasing club-head speed—and you don't get more club-head speed by generating more effort.

Three things give us distance: club-head speed, center-face hits, and correct angle of approach. So if you're pursuing power by increasing effort instead of making these three elements work in harmony, you are going down the wrong road—and it won't take you as far down the fairway as you want.

A better way to pursue distance is the way that Davis Love, Jr., taught Davis III. Father would have son make a full, complete swing with the driver but try to hit his ball only 100 yards. Then he'd have him take a full swing and hit it 150. Another swing, 200 yards. Then 250. Finally, Davis Jr. would let Davis III swing at the last ball as hard as he could, which, as you can imagine, often produced a pretty extraordinary result, but just as often produced a rocket that went into the wrong galaxy.

The idea was for Davis III to learn how to make his body back off and move in sync with his arms and club. He learned to increase his club-head speed, not his physical effort. And he learned to control his power rather than let the pursuit of it control him.

The hands and the wrists put the club in the right arc. The arms put the swing in the correct routing. The body responds in harmony with the swing.

○ ○ ○

SWING THOUGHTS . . .

Golfers frequently ask me to give them a "swing thought," a key to guide them during the swing. I'm generally reluctant to do so because I don't want you running through a mental checklist at precisely the moment you should be giving yourself over to athletic habits.

But the mind doesn't become a void during the golf swing, and sometimes it helps to have a single, centered thought, one idea that encompasses a lot of things. Maybe about the target ("straight at the tall pine"). Maybe about the body ("soft right hand"). Not one thought works for everyone. Always make it positive. "Don't hit it in the water" is the best prescription I know for hitting it straight in the water. Some good golfers don't like to have backswing thoughts at all; if they do have a swing thought, it's about the forward swing ("Keep spine angle"). Most good golfers play best when their minds are on the target—they might try to visualize square club-head–ball contact. Whatever it is, keep your swing thought simple.

I suppose I can't get out of here without giving you a swing thought, so here's a suggestion: "tempo." Break it into two syllables if you like: "tem" on the way back and "po" as you change directions. Or save it for the top—"tem-po"—and use it to trigger your change of direction.

. . . AND *PRE*-SWING THOUGHTS

To be truthful, I'm much more interested in your *pre*-swing thoughts, an idea or two that you incorporate into your Pre-Shot Routine or thoughts that guide your work

- Maintaining the proper spine angle throughout the swing relieves you of the need to manipulate the club head at impact.

- Feel the weight and position of the club head throughout your entire golf swing.
- Return hands and club to starting position and let momentum finish the swing.

SCORECARD SUMMARY

GRIP

- Hold club in fingers, not down in palms.
- Strong left hand: see two, perhaps three knuckles.
- V's formed by thumb and first finger on each hand as it grips club point to spot between chin and right shoulder.
- Light pressure: fingers secure, arms relaxed.
- Waggle club to relax arms and feel club head.

POSTURE

- Use eyes to confirm target line and align club face.
- Feel as if standing tall, back straight, chin up.
- Bend at hips.
- Flex slightly at knees so arms can hang freely.
- Tilt torso slightly to right.
- Weight on balls of feet.
- Track eyes along target line.

SWING

- Key concept: *Let swinging of arms and club turn body.*
- Blend use of feet and legs for support.
- Feel swing as pendulum-like for rhythm and balance.
- The game is about feel and sensitivity, not about power.
- Let the air out of your arms at the change of direction.
- Maintain spine angle through impact and finish.
- Apply club head to the ball.

LESSON 7

GLANCE AT THE BALL . . . *LOOK* AT THE TARGET

NINE OUT OF TEN GOLFERS put themselves in a hole before they even draw the club back. How? By not aiming at the target.

Hard to believe? Sure is—but it's only too true. Of the golfers who come through the Nicklaus-Flick Golf School, and I do believe they represent a pretty good cross section, only 10 percent or so set up with the correct alignment—aiming dead at the target. Another 10 percent or so aim to the left, most of them because they've given up on trying to cure a big slice and have resigned themselves to playing with it. But the vast majority, approximately 80 percent, aim to the right of the target.

Ask any of the tour players about the number one setup-and-aim flaw of their amateur partners in the pro-ams, and you'll get a virtually unanimous answer: they aim to the right of the target.

I believe I know what you're thinking. Something on the order of "That's pretty shocking. But it sure doesn't apply to me. I'll bet a sleeve of golf balls on it."

Maybe you really are one of the 10 percent who set up with the correct alignment. But I'm still going to take that bet.

There's just one problem: my garage isn't big enough to hold all those golf balls.

YOU'RE IN GOOD COMPANY

Let me tell you a Jack Nicklaus story that will illuminate the importance of aim and alignment.

It took place at the 1996 Tradition, one of the Senior Tour's four majors. The tournament is played at Desert Mountain in Scottsdale, Arizona, where many of the Nicklaus-Flick Golf School sessions are conducted during late winter and spring. Jack arrived in Scottsdale late Tuesday after playing a match for Shell's *Wonderful World of Golf* TV series against Lee Trevino in Mexico, where, Jack told me, he'd played "just lousy."

I hadn't worked with him in a while, so we'd arranged to get together the following morning before the tournament began on Thursday. The plan was to spend some time on the practice tee, then play a practice round.

Jack's problem, he told me, was that he didn't know where his ball was going off the tee. Everybody knows that Jack plays a high fade. And there have been very few more accurate long drivers in the game. But sure enough, here he was pulling three or four straight, then leaving the ball way right of where he wanted. Everything's relative, of course—Jack's standards are pretty doggone high. He wasn't happy.

After watching him about five minutes, I asked him to take his stance for a shot but not take the club back. I stepped up, put my right foot next to his, and slid it into exactly the same place his right foot had been. Then I stepped over, did the same thing with my left foot, took his driver, and asked him to go stand behind the ball, along the target line, where I'd been.

"Tell me, Jack," I asked, "where would you think a golfer aligned this way would be likely to hit the ball?"

"Oh, my goodness, Jim," he said. "From there he'd hit the ball thirty yards right."

Within five minutes, Jack was hitting those long, high left-to-right drives that have been his signature since he was at Ohio State—and he was hitting them exactly where he wanted to. Then we went out for the practice round: same result. That weekend he finished 65–65 and won the Tradition for the fourth time.

Now, Jack would have figured this problem out, probably sooner than later. No golfer on earth knows more about the golf swing, no golfer is more analytical, no golfer understands better that golf is a game requiring constant adjustments than Jack Nicklaus.

The moral of the story is that if Jack Nicklaus, the greatest golfer who ever played the game, can develop a problem with his aim and alignment serious enough to hamper his game, then where does that leave the rest of us?

Needing to think a lot more about aim and alignment, that's where.

> **"Once your mind knows you've mis-aimed, your body gives up on making a good swing."**
>
> **—Frank Beard**

POP QUIZ: DEFINE "PARALLEL"

What do you mean, "define 'parallel' "? Everybody knows what parallel means. Two lines, equidistantly apart at every point, that never meet (except in modern physics, where they meet in infinity).

Okay, if you got that right, you passed with flying colors. But now I want you to *demonstrate* parallel. Stand up behind your ball, nice and tall, and hold your arms straight out in front of you, right arm pointing through the ball to the target, left arm parallel to the right arm.

I do this with every group of golfers I teach, and I have to report the flunk-out rate is astounding. Sure, everybody *knows* what parallel means, but when I ask golfers to hold their arms out parallel in front of them, most people hold their arms out with their hands about a foot apart. Their arms are *not* parallel. They're converging at the target.

Okay, you may be thinking, so what?

Just this: the reason so many golfers mis-aim to the right of their target is that they mistake convergence for parallel.

THE CONCEPT OF PARALLEL LEFT

Find yourself a nice, long stretch of train track going straight out over really flat land—Kansas will do. Now go stand in between the tracks, look as far as you can down the line, and tell me what you see. It looks as if the tracks meet, I'll grant you that. But do they? They'd better not. But your eyes sure make you think they do.

Back home at your practice range, go stand *behind* your golf ball and look straight toward your target. That's your target line, agreed? If golf were like billiards and you set up to hit your ball from behind it, aim and alignment wouldn't be so tricky. But it's not, so they are.

Here's why. Take your normal stance—good posture, fingers secure, arms relaxed—and look straight at your target. Now, if you were to line up square to that line of sight—and by square,

I mean that a club shaft laid against your toes, your thighs, and your chest would point straight down the line between your eyes and your target—well, that would be 100 percent perfect aim and alignment, wouldn't it?

Yes, but only if you're interested in hitting your ball about twenty yards right of your target.

The reason aim and alignment are so tricky for most golfers—and why 80 percent aim too far to the right—is that you *swing at a golf ball from a position three feet or so to the side of the target line, not on it.* If your body is aligned square to a straight line from your eyes to the target, then your club face is going to be aligned square to a straight line from your ball to a spot well to the right of your target—the longer the shot, the more to the right your target line will extend.

The correct alignment for most golfers is parallel left, that is, body square to a line running parallel and to the left of the target line. Now, it's true that a lot of good players deviate from parallel left—Lee Trevino, for example, sets up well to the left of it. But I know of very few good golfers who consistently set up to the *right* of parallel left.

If you've been setting up too much to the right—that is, if you're among the Misaligned Majority—then parallel left is going to seem strange. You're going to feel as if your stance is way too open because now your body is set left of the target, not converging on the target. And your body will begin to creep back to the old, comfortable, right-of-target alignment that contributes to all sorts of problems, from pull-hooks to pushes to flat-out slices, especially when you leave the practice range and go out on the golf course, where the familiar feels better, even when it's dead wrong.

Your ability to aim is no better than the consistency of your habit of establishing and using your target line. People who

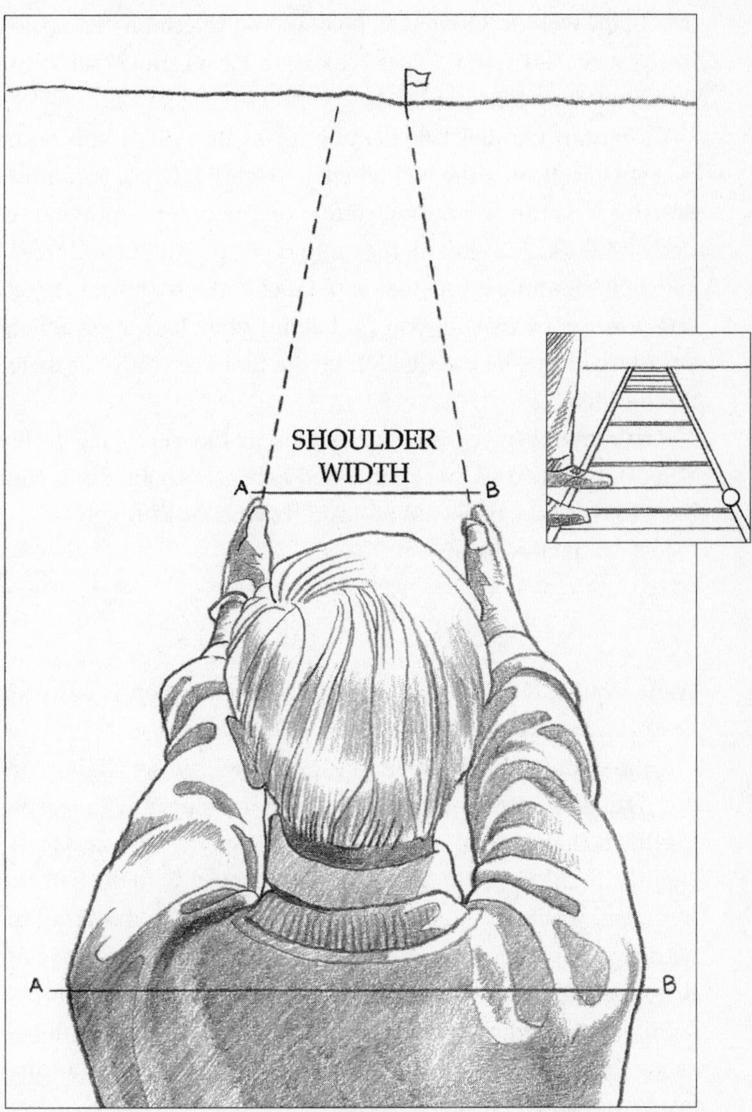

Optical Illusion. Train tracks look as if they converge, but they don't. Keep that in mind when setting up parallel left of the target line for a shot.

don't aim well don't want to be bothered to establish a target line, much less use it. That makes about as much sense as throwing darts blindfolded.

To ingrain parallel left, the alignment that gives you your best shot at putting the ball where you want it to go, you must practice it. Set up a learning station on the practice range (see Lesson 13). Place a club on the ground just in front of your feet, and point it along a line that is parallel and left of your target line. On the course, as you go behind your ball to establish your target line, let parallel left be the first item on your mental checklist.

And remember: correct alignment is *not* like riding a bicycle. You can forget. You can slip into bad habits. It's something you have to work on, be aware of—and fix when it's broken.

Just ask Jack Nicklaus.

SEEING IS BELIEVING

Want a quick check on whether your ball position is correct? Look down and tell me what part of the ball you see.

If I'm going to hit a driver, I've got my weight set slightly on my right side, with the ball forward in my stance. The reason for that is that my ball is on a tee, and I want the club face to be slightly on the upswing when it makes contact with the ball. So if my ball position and body setup are correct for the shot I'm getting ready to make, my right eye should be looking dead at the back of the ball, my left eye catching a little bit of the top.

But if I'm hitting an iron, I see more of the top of the ball because the ball's back toward the middle of my stance and my head's not as far back.

When I'm hitting a chip shot, with the ball well back in my stance and my weight shifted to my left side, I see more of the front of the ball with my left eye than with my right eye—just the reverse of what I see when hitting a driver.

MULTIPLE TARGETS

You set up to the ball aligned perfectly, parallel left. Now, where is your target? Well, it's out there—that piece of fairway 220 yards away, that half of the green 145 yards away, whatever. Fine, but isn't that a long way? Wouldn't it be easier if you had something closer in?

Most tour players—indeed, most really good players—pick intermediate points along their target line to guide their eyes. The intermediate targets can be a clump of dirt, a divot, a twig—just about anything that will reinforce their commitment to a swing path that delivers the ball to its ultimate target.

Jack Nicklaus uses four intermediate targets. One is just a few inches in front of him, so he can see it in his peripheral vision when he's looking down at the ball. Another is some twelve to fifteen feet in front of him and a third maybe thirty to forty yards down the fairway. And Jack even uses one behind the ball to help delineate his swing line when he takes the club back.

When you see him turning his head forward and back, forward and back, as he addresses his ball, it's not because he's trying to work out a crick in his neck. He's locking in on his intermediate targets.

○ ○ ○

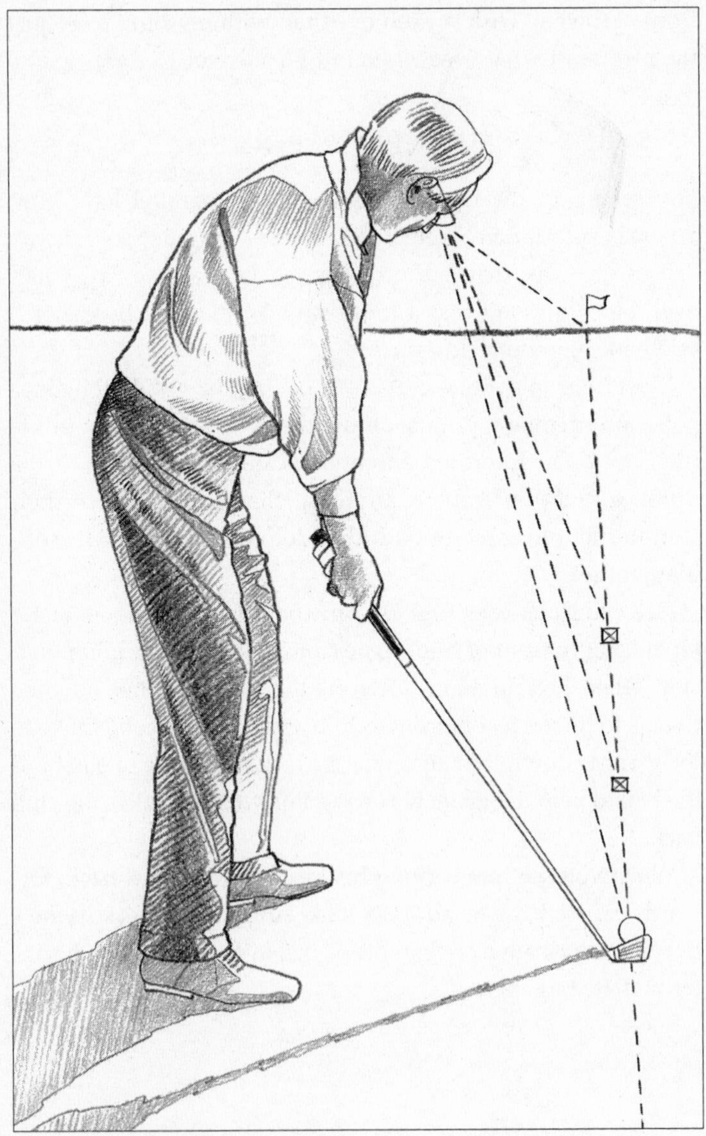

Don't Settle for One. Multiple intermediate targets make for better aim.

"KEEP YOUR EYE ON THE BALL"

That's what we were all told when we were learning the game. But why? The ball's not going anywhere.

Watch what good players do with their eyes when they address the ball. They spend relatively little time staring down at the ball. They're looking at the *target*. The ball's going to be there when they're ready to hit it, so the number one thing they're concerned about is the target. That's the image they want to hold in their mind.

If you spend more time looking at your ball than looking at your target, you may learn a lot about dimple architecture and grass, but you won't learn much about playing golf.

LOVE AFFAIR

Frank Beard, a longtime member of the PGA Tour and a thoughtful student of the game, once said, "A good player falls in love with his target."

I can only add that it is a love you should never forsake.

SCORECARD SUMMARY

- Number one flaw: aim too far to right.
- Concept of parallel left: align body square to line running parallel and to left of target line.
- Create multiple intermediate targets to lock in aim.
- At address, spend more time looking at target than ball.
- Key Concept: *Fall in love with your target.*

LESSON 8

STRICTLY ROUTINE

READY FOR SOME REALLY good news? Try this on for size: *Most of the things that contribute to a bad shot in golf occur before you begin your backswing.*

That's terrific, isn't it? Ranks right up there with the IRS discovering an error in your favor, the weatherman being wrong about the rain forecast for Saturday, and the Super Bowl actually turning out to be a good football game.

What it means is that there is something you can do *before* you swing your club that will dramatically increase your chances of being happy *after* you swing it. What you do is put a good Pre-Shot Routine in place.

The rock-solid foundation upon which every good golf shot rests is the Pre-Shot Routine. The pros know this. Most amateurs don't seem to.

Next time you get a chance, go to a pro tournament—a regular tour, LPGA, or Seniors event; it doesn't matter—and follow some of the better players around. You can pick up a lot more useful information watching them in the flesh than on TV. Not so much about their swings, which are the end product of thousands of hours of training, development, refinement, *and* a high level of natural athletic ability, but about a lot of other things that are eminently transferable to your own game.

For instance, you can learn how the pros use the range—that is, how they warm *up* for a round and *practice* after it. You can learn how they conduct themselves on the course—how they respond to bad shots and good ones, bad breaks and lucky breaks. And, most important, you can see them prepare carefully for each shot with their Pre-Shot Routine.

That routine will vary from pro to pro, of course. Some are methodical, even painstaking. Others are so rapid-fire there doesn't seem to be any routine at all. (Trust me, there is.) And there will be variations, depending on the type and difficulty of the shot. But each routine includes a checklist that the pro goes through, out of ingrained habit rather than conscious choice, before he draws the club back.

One reason the Pre-Shot Routine is important is obvious: the only time to assess your lie, factor in such conditions as wind and topography, select the right club, take aim, align yourself properly, and set the correct grip pressure is *before* you swing. You have a pre-shot checklist for the same reason that an airline pilot has a pre-flight checklist—you don't want to forget anything that might lead your shot to crash and burn. A good Pre-Shot Routine can't make every swing perfect, but it can help you get the best out of every swing, good or bad, that you make.

But there is another critically important reason for creating, practicing, and internalizing your own Pre-Shot Routine: it helps condition your conscious mind to give way, to give in, and to stop trying to control or manipulate the smooth functioning of your swinging and turning elements. You hear a lot about how people ought to get in touch with their feelings. I don't quite know how that works in human relations, but I have a pretty good idea how it works in golf.

GOOD HABITS EARN GOOD SHOTS

Developing habits is kind of like putting eggs in a basket: the first egg that falls out is the last one put in place. That's the way it is with habits: the first habit you lose is the last one you've worked on because you haven't had it long enough.

A habit doesn't get formed because your mind announces one day that, henceforth and forevermore, I am always going to check my grip pressure before every shot. A habit forms because you perform a certain action over and over, so much so that it becomes second nature: you don't have to create a set of conscious mind-to-body commands to perform it.

When you brush your teeth in the morning, do you consciously itemize all the sequential components of that action—take the toothbrush from the holder, remove the toothpaste from the medicine cabinet, unscrew the cap, and so on? Of course not. You just do it. The component actions are ingrained. They are, in effect, preprogrammed. They constitute a habit—one you've had so long that it's not likely to fall out of the basket.

So much of success in golf depends on habit formation. If you form good habits, then good shots seem to happen, even when you're not expecting them, because those habits help you create consistency. You don't get better by consciously commanding yourself to make a better shot. You improve because you've developed good habits, and good habits earn good shots.

A Pre-Shot Routine consists of a lot of good habits packaged together. If you take your Pre-Shot Routine seriously, practice it, and truly make it an integral part of your game, you will earn many more good shots.

PRE-SHOT ROUTINE: THE BASICS

The first moments I spend with a student on the golf course are always revealing. I get to see how he approaches the game, as play or work, and how he manages success and failure. And I almost always identify a way to help him with his game immediately—*without touching his golf swing*. How? I help him develop the habit of going through a well-constructed Pre-Shot Routine.

A Pre-Shot Routine is a personal thing. Billy Casper's routine starts when he takes his club out of the bag. Part of Corey Pavin's routine is his squirrelly-looking rehearsal swing that looks like a hand-me-down from a twenty handicapper and has no resemblance whatsoever to the swing he actually puts on the ball. Some good golfers are methodical. Some play so they don't seem to have any routine at all. But they do.

Once established, your Pre-Shot Routine should not vary, good round or bad. Nobody's better at that than Jack Nicklaus. He will not back down, will not alter his routine when things are going bad. Many golfers, when things go bad, give up, drop their routines. But when they do that, they're not putting themselves in the position to let good habits take over. A good, solid Pre-Shot Routine should be an anchor in good times and bad.

Whatever the whims of individual golfers, all good routines have certain elements in common. I'm going to construct a model Pre-Shot Routine on a dozen of those elements. I'm not saying you have to follow each of these steps in exact order. But I am saying you should consider them in developing your own routine.

1. Inspect Your Lie

Okay, here's the situation. You have exactly 150 yards to the center of the green. All you have to do is put the ball in the middle of the green, make two putts, and you're the U.S. Open champion. Now, what club are you going to use?

Seven iron.

You sure?

Yep. Seven is my 150-yard club. Most reliable club in my bag. Love my seven iron.

Even though your ball is sitting down in four-inch rough, on a sidehill lie, below your feet?

Oh, so it is . . .

An exaggeration? Not by much. What kind of lie you have is the first thing you should take into consideration in planning a shot. But for too many golfers, it's the *last* thing they notice—and that's when they're standing over the ball.

Remember: the first thing you always do is inspect your lie. Everything else follows from the results of that inspection.

2. Assess Conditions

A lot of things affect what happens to your ball when it reaches the target area. You need to factor in the topography—is the target area flat, sloping left or right, uphill or downhill? You need to factor in potential trouble—out of bounds, bunkers, water—and identify alternate routes to your target. You need to factor in the best place to miss your shot—if there's water just left of the green, you want to construct a shot that, if it misses, misses right. And, of course, you need to factor in the wind.

The wind is one condition that every golfer factors in to some degree, and for an obvious reason: he feels it. The problem is "to some degree" hides three fairly huge variables. How much wind is there? Where's it coming from? (Not as easy to determine as it might seem.) How's it going to affect which club I use?

The 123-yard seventh hole at Pebble Beach, perched picturesquely on a little spit of land jutting out into the Pacific Ocean, is the shortest par three the PGA Tour regularly visits. But it's also one of the most treacherous because the wind can range from barely a zephyr (easy sand wedge for the pros) to brisk (full nine iron) to what-in-the-hell-are-we-doing-out-here (try to punch a five iron under it and hope for the best). Direction is not a problem: it's always in your face. Velocity is.

Probably the most famous par three in golf is the twelfth at Augusta National, the hole at Amen Corner that has, at one time or another, brought most of the world's great golfers to their knees. It's a fairly wide green, but very shallow, and the back-to-front slope leads right down a well-clipped bank to a pond. (The bank is where Freddie Couples's ball miraculously stopped in the final round when he won the 1992 Masters. The pond is where Greg Norman's ball drowned in the final round when he lost the 1996 Masters.) What makes the twelfth at Augusta so devilishly challenging, of course, is the famous Sunday pin placement (well to the right, inviting golfers to meet the fate that Norman suffered and Couples averted) and the importance of the hole in the Masters. ("He can't win it here," Ken Venturi said, as Norman stepped up to the tee, "but he can sure lose it here." He did.)

The wind, given the delicate nature of the shot from 155 yards, obviously becomes a major factor in club selection. But here the big question is not how hard the wind is blowing but where it's blowing from. The twelfth hole at Augusta is located at the base of a hill, protected from the wind by tall trees both behind the green and up higher on the hill where the tee is located. So what happens is that the wind swirls. A golfer not familiar with Augusta might feel a breeze in his face on the tee, select his club accordingly, then discover when his ball's in flight that up high, above tree level, the wind is blowing dead straight at the hole.

Local legend has it that Ben Hogan always used to look back at the flagstick on the eleventh green, about seventy-five yards to the left of the twelfth tee. Whichever way the flag was blowing, he'd figure just the opposite in planning his shot. No wonder the twelfth hole has shattered so many Masters dreams over the years.

Now, am I going into such detail to prepare you for making birdies on the seventh at Pebble Beach and the twelfth at Augusta National? No. (Although I'll tip my cap to you if you do.) The point I'm trying to make here is that something so simple as which way the wind is blowing isn't always as simple after all.

3. See Your Shot

Until this point of your Pre-Shot Routine, everything's been based on conscious use of your mind. You've been using your conscious mind to collect and evaluate data, all for the purpose of deciding on the type of shot you want to make and the club you want to make it with.

But once you've made your club selection, the focus of your Pre-Shot Routine shifts. Now you summon the *feel* of the shot that you're preparing to play. And the first step in doing that is to see your shot before you make it.

Go back behind the ball and look down your target line. I want you to see your shot. Really see it. Don't see your swing—I don't want you to be distracted by mechanical thoughts. See your *shot.* Shut out everything else. See your ball climbing on its trajectory, isolated against the sky, and descending into your target zone. See it land, bounce, and roll toward the flag.

Don't think about it.

See it.

4. Select Your Instrument

The last element I like to consider before selecting a club is distance. I don't like putting distance first because there's a tendency to commit subconsciously to a club that may not fit the conditions of the shot.

The club you select is going to depend on your own skill level and your own experience. For some golfers, 150 yards with no wind is an easy eight iron, for others a hard six iron, while for most it's probably a smooth seven. Doesn't matter one whit. You don't get style points for reaching the green with an easy five iron while the other guys in your foursome are getting there with hard four irons.

Too many golfers base their club selection exclusively on a fond memory of a career shot with that particular instrument. Positive reinforcement is one thing; self-delusion is another. Take a club that will put the ball in the target zone with your 80 percent swing—that is, your normal swing, not one that requires all the stars in the universe to be aligned just so.

I'm not recommending timidity here. I'm recommending that you take into account how you're swinging and how you're feeling about yourself and your talent level. If you're swinging well and feeling confident, you can afford to be a little aggressive. If not, then back off a tad. Don't let a random macho impulse obscure your objective judgment: excessive effort too often creates out-of-control golf swings.

It *sometimes* makes good sense to play aggressively, but it *always* makes good sense to play smart.

The worst thing that can happen if you make a drop-dead perfect swing and your ball goes too far is usually not too bad—in newer courses, for instance, much of the trouble around most of the greens is in front and on the sides, not behind. On the other hand, the worst thing that can happen if you choose a club that requires a perfect swing and then make only an average swing . . . well, does the sound "Splash!" sound familiar?

When in doubt, take more club.

5. Lock On

Now that you know what your shot's going to look like, lock onto your target. This is paramount. It must become your obsession. Don't think about your takeaway or your backswing. Don't let your conscious mind interfere.

How you use your mind at this juncture has a crucial effect on your tension level. When you talk to yourself—that is, when you let your conscious mind direct your swing—you create tension in your body, especially in your hands and forearms. When you let your swing be guided by a picture of your target, there is no such tension buildup.

Give up all mechanical thoughts and turn yourself over, body and soul, to your target.

6. "Feel Your Club Head"

First, hold the club straight up, pointing to the sky, and feel the weight of the club head—too light.

Next, hold the club straight out from your body, parallel to the ground, and feel the weight of the club head—too heavy.

Now hold the club at a 45-degree angle (between parallel to the ground and straight up), and "Feel the Weight of the Club Head"—just right.

This is critical. If you can't "Feel Your Club Head," you probably won't feel your swing.

7. Take a Rehearsal Swing

Most golfers take a swing before they step up to make their shot. That's fine—just don't think of it as a "practice swing." You're not "practicing" anything. You're *rehearsing*.

If you take a rehearsal swing and feel uncomfortable or off balance, it's usually because your effort level was excessive. Take another, this time focusing on tempo, rhythm, and balance.

Your rehearsal swing should prepare you for the shot you are getting ready to play, so make sure you set up for it looking down the target line—either from behind the ball or beside it—the way you'll be when you take your for-real swing.

8. Square Your Club Face to the Target

Your eyes are locked onto your target. Next comes your club face. Holding your club straight out and parallel to the ground, make sure your club face is perpendicular to the ground—neither closed nor open. Now, with your eyes fixed on the target line, walk up to your ball and position the club head behind the ball so that its face is exactly perpendicular to the target line you have so carefully established.

9. Fit Your Stance to Your Club

Your club face is in position behind the ball, square to the target line. It's time now to adjust your stance to fit the club. Without moving your club, step into place, close enough to your ball to reach it comfortably without stretching, far enough away so that your arms can hang and swing freely. Adjust your feet so that your legs give solid support to your body and arms.

Remember: first fit your club to your ball, then your stance to your club—never vice versa.

10. Posture!

Feet at shoulder-width. Bend at hips. Back straight, but tilted slightly forward. Gently flex knees. On balls of your feet. Feel hamstrings supporting your body. Make sure arms have space to swing freely under your shoulder sockets. That's all second nature, right? No need to think about it? That's good. Now, just one more thing: make sure you can breathe.

Sports physiologists say that the more oxygen you have in your system, the more relaxed your muscles can be. That's why deep, full breaths are a part of any free-throw shooter's or field-goal kicker's routine. Singers, dancers, and even TV announcers know the importance of full oxygenation—deep breaths, in golfer's lingo—before they have to perform.

If you bury your chin in your chest, you will block your left shoulder from turning in response to your backswing, and you will restrict your breathing. So: shoulders back, chin up—and breathe.

11. Waggle

Most good golfers waggle. They may waggle differently—Ray Floyd's waggle is virtually a signature; you'd never mistake it for anyone else's—but they waggle.

The waggle has two specific purposes: to get tension out of your arms and hands and to help you feel the club head in motion.

It's hard to waggle and tense up at the same time.

12. Deep Breaths, Long Looks

Deep breaths and long looks at the target make good sense throughout the Pre-Shot Routine. The deep breaths help relax you. The long looks focus your eyes on the target and commit your subconscious to the task. Now, just before liftoff, how about one more deep breath and one more long look? You'll find the number that fits your routine best.

FORWARD PRESS

You're fully prepared to make a golf swing. How do you begin it?

Sounds like a silly question, but it isn't. Everything in the Pre-Shot Routine has brought you to a state of readiness, but you need a trigger to initiate the golf swing, to spark the change from a state of preparation to a state of execution. And, to promote consistency, it needs to be the same trigger before every full swing. It's both a bridge and a catalyst.

Some good players literally press their hands forward slightly, then begin their backswing. Others cock their heads almost imperceptibly. Tom Kite says he scrunches his toes up inside his shoes. Whatever you do, it shouldn't be abrupt.

The forward press is either the last stage of the Pre-Shot Routine or the first stage of the swing—take your pick. Just don't forget to find your own trigger.

> **Good golfers *train* by analyzing and thinking. They *play* by feeling and seeing.**

THIS IS GOLF, NOT THE ARMY

Do you have to follow every single part of the Pre-Shot Routine I just outlined in exact order? No. I do think you should take all those components into account, and I do think you should restrict the analytical-cognitive elements to the beginning of your routine. But the more personal your routine is and the more it reflects your thinking about it, the more likely you are to follow it on the golf course.

TIME MANAGEMENT

Oh, this is great! As if the five-hour round weren't bad enough, now Flick comes along and wants to add another half hour to it so everybody can go through a seventy-three-point checklist on every shot. No, thanks!

Not so. I think slow play is just about the worst thing about the game of golf today, and I'm not in favor of anything that makes it slower.

A lot goes into a carefully worked out Pre-Shot Routine, but the routine doesn't take up a lot of time—thirty seconds, maybe less, *once it becomes a habit*. In fact, it helps you use the time setting up for a shot more efficiently. You know precisely what you need to do; you don't have to waste time thinking, Did I do this or did I do that?

The less time you take in your Pre-Shot Routine—*without skipping any steps*—the better. You do *not* want to become static in preparing to make your shot.

Trouble shots—from the woods or from any really difficult lie—will necessarily take more prep time. Once you step up to your ball, though, proceed at your usual pace. You've got trouble enough without letting a lot of heavy thinking interfere with the naturalness of your swing.

And when you have a good lie in the fairway, go through your routine quickly (but completely) and get on with your shot.

As Tom Watson says, "Long means wrong."

PRACTICE MY *WHAT?*

The average golfer knows that it's a pretty good idea to have a Pre-Shot Routine—maybe he heard it on TV, or maybe he read it in some book. Goodness knows I can't think of anything that's given more lip service. But if I go up to that average golfer on a practice range and ask how much time he spends working on his Pre-Shot Routine, he's going to look at me as if I'd just dropped in from Mars. He just wants to hit some more balls.

Now, I've got a problem with that approach. The only other place to work on a routine is on the golf course. And if he has to create a routine and practice it on the golf course, when is he going to have time to play the game?

Your Pre-Shot Routine can't be truly yours unless you practice it—and there's only one place for that. I'm not saying you have to go through your full routine before every shot on the practice range. But I do say that on a designated number of full-swing shots, using different clubs and assorted targets, you should go through your full routine. That reinforces its importance, confirms your commitment to it, and makes you more likely to follow it on the golf course, where it will do your game a world of good.

ROUND MOUND ROUTINE

Everybody knows Charles Barkley is a passionate golfer, but he's also pretty good at another sport. Watch him—or any good foul shooter—at the free-throw line. He looks at the basket, then he spins the ball up and catches it in his hands lightly to feel its weight. He does that a precise number of times, always bringing his eyes up to focus on the basket. Then he bounces the ball to help relax his arms. Then he brings the ball back to eye level and he's up and gone. He does it every time the same way. He's not thinking about what to do because he's done it so many times. It's a habit. It's a trigger for him that shuts out crowd noise and thoughts about the score.

He has a pretty good Pre-Shot Routine in golf, too.

FUNNEL VISION

In life, you always want to see the big picture—you don't want to see the trees but miss the forest. Peripheral vision is essential for point guards, NASCAR drivers, and running backs. Hindsight works for all of us. A panoramic view can be breathtaking, particularly from your own backyard.

But on the golf course, I want you to have funnel vision.

Make your eyes aware of one thing and one thing only: the target. Looking side to side—seeing the OB stakes on the left and the trees on the right—only plants seeds of doubt in your golf swing before you take the club back. Let your eyes track down the target line so that your vision funnels into the target. That's why I want you to leave a club along your target line when practicing—to encourage proper use of your eyes.

There will be plenty of time to take in the scenery between shots.

KEEP YOUR MOUTH SHUT

Do *not* verbalize during your Pre-Shot Routine. Don't tell yourself, I'm going to do this, I'm going to do that. And for sure don't tell yourself, I'm *not* going to do this or that, as in "I'm not going to pull-hook the ball into the pond on the left." Give yourself over to seeing your ball flying through the air directly at your target.

USE YOUR HEAD . . .

Don't get me wrong: you have to think on the golf course.

You need to inspect your lie, evaluate conditions that affect your shot, identify the type of shot required, isolate the target, estimate the distance to it, then select the right club for the task of moving the ball to the target zone.

All those are conscious, cognitive actions. Ignore them at your peril.

. . . BUT DON'T LET YOUR MIND INTERFERE

The purpose of your Pre-Shot Routine is to help your conscious mind surrender its control of your swing to your subconscious. You want to condition your conscious mind to give way to your subconscious—or, if you prefer, to your athletic habits. You want to eliminate cognitive interference with the smooth functioning of your swinging and turning elements.

Your Pre-Shot Routine begins with evaluation and analysis, then shifts to the repetition, in sequence, of certain noncognitive actions that should become second nature to you. If you have to ask yourself what to do next, then you haven't worked on your routine enough.

I want you to get to the point where you put about as much conscious effort into the individual components of your routine as you do into the individual steps involved in brushing your teeth.

○ ○ ○

THE ROUTINE: DON'T FORGET IT

1. Inspect lie.
2. Assess conditions.
3. See your shot.
4. Select instrument.
5. Lock on.
6. Feel your club head.
7. Take rehearsal swing.
8. Square club face to target.
9. Fit stance to club.
10. Posture!
11. Waggle.
12. Deep breaths, long looks.

POST-SHOT ROUTINE

Post-Shot? Hey, that train's left the station. How can any routine I follow *after* a shot be of any help? For better or worse, that ball's on its way.

True enough, but wouldn't you like a little feedback on your swing? If you get a positive result, you should have some idea what produced it. And with a negative result, you should learn all you can so you can fix it on the Training Ground.

So, after you hit the ball, hold your finish position until the ball strikes the ground. If you're comfortable and in balance, you know that your swinging pace is in sync. If you're teetering around trying to *get* your balance, you know that your swinging pace is out of sync. Not always, but usually an out-of-balance finish means there was a surge in effort level in an attempt to generate more power or control.

You really can learn something useful from your finish, so why not hold it for a few seconds, until your ball confirms the results of your swing?

Besides, if you hit a really *great* shot, you want to be in a good pose for the cameras.

❍ ❍ ❍

SCORECARD SUMMARY

- Establish a good Pre-Shot Routine—and stick to it.
- Use your Pre-Shot Routine as a bridge between conscious control and athletic performance.
- On course, have funnel vision.
- Key Concept: *Good habits earn good shots.*

LESSON 9

THE MONEY SHOT

AT THE END OF EACH Nicklaus-Flick Golf School, we have our version of the Ryder Cup. First we pair up the students into twosomes, balancing them according to experience and ability. Then we play a six-hole, two-person scramble, short-game tournament—two putts (one long, one medium), two chips, one pitch, and a bunker shot. Par is twelve.

We also play an extra hole—a shot to a green from sixty yards away. Hit it onto the green and you lower your team's net score by a stroke. The shots from both partners count: if both hit it on the green, the team's net score is reduced by two. Most of the twosomes are bunched around thirteen–fourteen after regulation play. So, considering the huge prize at stake—a couple of sleeves of balls—that extra hole is a big deal.

I should explain that a solid majority of the students who come to the Nicklaus-Flick Golf School play to handicaps somewhere in the twelve to twenty-eight range. A few have lower handicaps, a few higher, but most of our golfers score in the eighties and nineties. A pretty good cross section of America's golfers, in other words.

Would you care to guess how many hit the green from sixty yards out on that extra hole in the Nicklaus-Flick Cup matches? About one in three.

Some people call it the "half wedge." Others refer to it as the "part shot." Whatever the name, I say the shot you have to make fifty to sixty yards from the green—the shot that the average golfer, who doesn't consistently hit par fours and fives in regulation, is faced with about six to eight times a round—is one of the hardest shots in golf.

THE MONEY SHOT

What makes the "money shot"—we need our own name for it, don't we?—so doggone tough?

Well, for starters it's a "between" shot. Not a little pitch or chip, not a full swing, but somewhere in between.

On a short pitch or chip from around the green, you have a forgiveness cushion. Even if you don't make a particularly good shot, you'll likely end up somewhere on the putting surface. But from sixty yards away, there is less margin for error.

On a full-swing shot, the average golfer has a pretty good idea of how far his ball is going to travel. You know, for example, that your seven iron is going to go about 145 to 155 yards, provided you put your usual swing on it. But a sixty-yard shot is in a no-man's-land for many golfers. Sure, a sand wedge can give you sixty yards, but that can be a risky choice from a tight lie, and you may not always want such a high-trajectory shot, particularly if there's any wind.

The main reason the money shot is such a challenge for so many people is that they have had it drilled into their heads that the golf swing is all about big muscles and mechanics and positions. But the money shot is, predominantly, a *feel* shot. How is anybody who is constantly worrying about turning his shoulders and driving his hips, as so many golfers are, going to be able to develop the feel and sensitivity needed to execute the sixty-yard shot?

I thought you'd never ask.

DON'T SWING HARDER OR EASIER—SWING LONGER OR SHORTER

The basic principles for the money shot—aim, correct posture, proper grip pressure—are identical to the basic principles of full-swing shots. Yes, you still use a pendulum-like swing with the club swinging in balance. The only essential difference is in the length of the swing. That's worth repeating: *the key to the money shot is the length of the swing.*

You have to be aware of what you are doing to execute the money shot. And how do you become aware? Right—you *practice.* But make sure you practice the right things. I see too many people pumping out full-swing shots on the practice range—hit a ball, roll another over before the first one lands, hit again—without any conscious awareness of what they're doing. On the golf course, you *want* to switch off your conscious mind and play the game. On the practice range, however, in order to form good habits, you want to be acutely aware of what you are doing.

The first time I ask a student to pick a target sixty yards away, put the ball on a tee, and pull out a seven or eight iron, I get some quizzical responses, like: "But I use a sand wedge from this distance."

Probably you do, and probably you will—on the course. But on the Training Ground, there is a larger agenda. Yes, you're trying to put your ball into the target zone, but you're also trying to develop your feel and sensitivity for the swinging force of the club head into the back of the ball. And as you move on to a different target—say, one hundred yards away—you're learning that what creates distance is not increased effort but the increased length of your swing. *For more distance, you don't swing harder, you swing your arms and club longer.*

Anyway, where is it written that you absolutely, positively, have to use only one club for a certain-length shot? Try selling that idea to Seve Ballesteros, whose imagination and creativity never let him be straitjacketed when it comes to club selection. Perhaps that had to do with learning to play golf as a boy with a cut-down three iron—the only club he had—that he used for every shot in the game. Over his career, he's been a master of creativity. From the same distance, Seve might use any one of a half-dozen clubs, depending on conditions—his lie, the wind, the terrain, and so forth—and on what his imagination tells him is the best way to put the ball close to the flagstick. Even now, when it seems his best golf is behind him, Seve's a delight to watch anywhere within one hundred yards of the flag, especially if he's in some sort of trouble. He has every shot in the book, plus a bunch nobody would dare write down because they are so unbelievable.

There's no trick to the sixty-yard shot. You're still using the same aim, posture, and swing shape as for the full-swing shot. It's strictly a question of feel. And feel in golf can be acquired, nurtured, and practiced—even if you didn't learn golf as a kid with a cut-down three iron. You can do it by working on the money shot.

TWO-MINUTE DRILL

You got caught in traffic, you wrote down the wrong tee time, you showed up without a time but the starter can squeeze you in with a threesome that's up at 10:12—whatever, you only have a few minutes before it's time to step up to the first tee.

What do you do to get ready?

Some people would advise you to go directly to the practice green—and I sure couldn't fault that advice, given the impact of putting on your score. But if you're pretty confident in your putter, let me suggest another way to spend those precious few minutes before teeing off:

Practice the money shot.

Go to the range, pick a target fifty to sixty yards away, and pull out a seven or eight iron. You're feeling rushed, your adrenaline is pumping, and you're a prime candidate for a grip-and-rip, swing-with-all-your-might, knock-the-dimples-off-the-ball first-tee fiasco.

There's no better prescription for calming you down, getting yourself collected, and causing you to focus on rhythm and balance, balance and rhythm, than a handful of smoothly executed shots to a target sixty yards away *using way too much club.* Finish off your warm-up with a few shots with the wedge you'd normally use from that distance. You'll need that shot out on the course, but it will also be a big help getting you ready for all your other shots as well.

The bottom line: if short on time, spend it practicing the money shot.

THE BEST MEDICINE

I have a confession to make. When I ask you to spend time working on the money shot, it's not just because I think it's superimportant for you to become accurate from sixty yards in. It is, and you will, but there is another huge benefit. The feel and sensitivity that you acquire, nurture, and practice with the money shot will help your entire game, from tee to green.

You'll need the same kind of feel and sensitivity for swing length with *all* your irons. You'll need them with your putter. And even—make that *especially*—with your driver.

The full swing, in my opinion, should be built around the feel and sensitivity that is at the heart of the money shot. That's why, when guys lose their golf swing—which is going to happen from time to time; that's the nature of the game—I find that working on short-game shots is the best prescription for getting back their feel for full-swing shots.

Have I sold you on the idea that sixty yards from the flagstick is a great place to build your golf game *and* a great place to fix it? If not, grab a seven iron—okay, take your wedges, too—and head out to a practice range. Start at sixty yards, but move down to thirty and up to seventy, then back to sixty. Hit teed-up seven irons to get your rhythm, then go to your wedges. Pretend you're Seve: use the "wrong" club on purpose. Trust me. You'll feel the impact of the money-shot drill almost immediately—on the golf course.

SCORECARD SUMMARY

- Key Concept: *Part shot from fifty to sixty yards out is golf's "money shot."*
- When warming up before playing, *always* devote time to sixty-yard shots, even if that's all you do.
- Money shot also helps develop feel needed for full-swing shots.

LESSON 10

AROUND THE GREEN

IF IT'S HAPPENED ONCE, it's happened a thousand times. At the beginning of a Nicklaus-Flick Golf School session on shots from around the green, I'll approach a student, toss a ball down, and some version of the following conversation takes place:

What club would you choose for this shot?

I always use an eight iron for chip shots.

Always?

Yep. It's my chipping club.

Oh, why is that?

Because I feel more comfortable with an eight iron.

And confident?

Yes, comfortable and confident.

That's fine, but let me ask you—is your ball always exactly the same distance from the edge of the green?

Well, no . . .

Is it always exactly the same distance from the pin?

Umm, no . . .

Do you always have exactly the same lie?

No, it varies . . .

Does the green always have exactly the same speed and degree of contour?

Of course not . . .

Okay, so let me get this straight. On chip shots from around the green, the distance you have to carry the ball to get to the fringe varies, the amount of green you have to work with varies, the speed and degree of contour vary, your lie varies—and yet one club is the best choice for all those shots?

Uhh . . .

I have a tip for you.

What's that?

Don't ever lose that club.

WHAT INSTRUMENT?

The fact is, a lot of golfers get so attached to a single "chipping club" that they just about ignore everything else about the shot they face: "If I'm around the green, I use my eight iron (or my sand wedge, or whatever), period. Next question?"

Okay, answer this: from anywhere else on the course—other than the green itself—would you always pull out the same club without first factoring in lie, distance, wind, topography, and potential trouble, such as water or bunkers—in other words, all the variables that might affect your shot?

I thought not.

A lot of variables need to be taken into account in selecting the proper instrument for *any* shot. But around the green, the precise identification of conditions becomes especially critical because the choice of an instrument best suited for the task can mean the difference between leaving your ball in the long grass (or dumping it in a trap) and saving par.

CHIP AND PITCH

These could be the names of a kid and his dog in a 1950s sitcom, but every golfer will recognize the sometimes vexing either/or option he faces every time his approach shot misses a green.

Do I want a low-trajectory shot that lands just on the edge of the green and rolls smartly to within gimme distance of the hole? Or a high-trajectory shot that lands softly near the flagstick and trickles to within gimme distance of the hole? Obviously, either result would be delightful—but which shot is more likely to achieve it?

The answer is always easy enough, provided you remember (and follow!) Greenside Formula Number 1: Low Shot = Low Risk, High Shot = High Risk. Davis Love, Jr., put it this way: "Minimum Air/Maximum Ground."

For the average golfer, there is no Formula Number 2.

THE CHIP

Here are the Eight Basics for the chip, a low-trajectory shot that hits on the green just in from the edge and rolls toward the flagstick. The less air time the better.

1. After inspecting your lie, select club that will deliver just enough trajectory to carry ball onto green about three feet beyond the collar. Likely choices: nine, eight, seven, or six.
2. Ball toward back of stance, just to the right of the sternum. The worse the lie, the farther back in stance.
3. Hands just ahead of ball at address *and* at impact. Grip pressure slightly tighter than normal.
4. Weight on left leg and foot.

5. Left eye sees front of ball at address.
6. Pendulum-like stroke. Arms and shoulders only; hands and wrists only react to weight of club head.
7. Strike ball with descending arc (as consequence of setup and ball position).
8. Don't be concerned with amount of follow-through. (Ground will often stop club in any case.)

THE PITCH

And here are the Eight Basics for the pitch, a high-trajectory shot that rolls only a short distance after landing. This is a necessary shot when there is trouble (a bunker, deep rough) between your ball and the green that precludes a chip.

1. After inspecting your lie, select club that will deliver just enough trajectory to carry ball to desired landing spot. Likely choices: sand wedge, loft wedge, pitching wedge.
2. Ball in middle of stance, underneath the sternum.
3. Hands even with ball at address and at impact.
4. Weight evenly distributed.
5. Right eye sees back of ball at address, left eye sees top of ball.
6. Pendulum-like stroke. Mainly arms, shoulders respond. Allow whatever minimal wrist cock results from length of swing and weight in club head.
7. Strike ball at bottom of swing arc.
8. Don't be concerned with amount of follow-through. With correct grip pressure and arm freedom, momentum will take care of it.

❍ ❍ ❍

"I'M TWENTY-FIVE YARDS FROM THE PIN. WHAT SHOULD I DO, CHIP OR PITCH?"

Sorry, you haven't given me enough information to answer that. Distance is only one factor. What about your lie? How close is the pin to the edge of the green—in other words, how much green do you have to work with? What is the contour of the green? Once you have this information, you can answer your own question: just go back to Greenside Formula Number 1. In case you've forgotten, I'll repeat it: Low Shot = Low Risk, High Shot = High Risk.

MONEY-SHOT ADVISORY

From a bad lie in deep rough, forget about the pitch shot: go ahead and use a lofted club, but play from a chip-shot setup.

If your ball is sitting down in deep grass, it's very difficult to play a standard pitch. With your hands positioned even with the ball, your club face can't get to the ball—hello, skull. You'll be tempted to try to scoop the ball out—hello, chili dip.

Rather than try to force a shot that's not suited to the lie, pick a lofted club—and hit a shot following the Chip Basics. The chipping stroke will get the club face through the grass, and the descending blow with the lofted club will pop the ball up and out more consistently.

SEE THE SHOT

A good free-throw shooter in basketball sees the ball arcing up, dropping down, and hitting nothing but net—*before* he turns the ball loose. He sees his shot before he takes it. But, compared to a golfer, the basketball player shooting a free throw has it easy: he's always shooting from the same distance, the rim is always ten feet from the floor, and wind is not a factor. Before a golfer can *see* his chip or pitch shot, he has to do a little *looking*.

One of the reasons we take students out onto the golf course the first day at the Nicklaus-Flick Golf School is to see how they react under normal playing conditions, and I'm always struck by the Pre-Shot Routine followed by most golfers around the green. That is, none at all.

Oh, they'll take a look at the lie—and that's really important. Whether the ball's sitting up nicely or burrowed down into the long grass dictates what kind of shot you have. But there's so much more you can learn, *need* to learn around the green, *if* you have a good, basic Pre-Shot Routine.

Inspect the lie, yes. But also walk onto the green and let your feet give you a sense of the firmness of the surface your ball's going to be hitting. To get a complete picture of the conditions you have to work with, take a look at your shot from the side, perhaps as you're walking up to the green. Evaluate the topography: uphill slope, downhill, flat? And, most important, *find out how much green you have to work with.*

Pick a landing spot and take a mental picture of the ball landing and rolling to the flagstick. Then take a rehearsal swing that relates to the distance your ball must travel in the air to reach the landing spot. You're rehearsing technique, yes, but you're primarily rehearsing the length of the swing needed to get your ball where you've decided it needs to land.

"SET YOUR MIND AT EASE SO YOUR BODY CAN PERFORM"

That was a favorite saying of Davis Love, Jr., a very dear friend and one of golf's great teachers. It's a wonderful thing to keep in mind for every shot in golf, but especially for the toughest ones. Let me illustrate.

You hit a strong approach shot but miss the green, you walk up to your ball, you check the lie, and then you look into the high, towering face of a huge, gaping bunker, with only the top half of the flagstick visible behind it.

What's the first thing that crosses your mind?

Sorry, conceding the hole is not acceptable, not so long as we're partners. Nor is a decision to wind up and hit a full wedge or something well over the flagstick and take your chances with whatever unseen hell awaits on the other side of the green—anything to avoid that bunker. And ticking off a mental checklist of "bunker basics" in anticipation of chunking your ball into that sandy face isn't exactly the confidence builder you need.

In seeking a safe landing spot, you need to ask a basic question—How much green do I have to work with?—the answer to which, far more often than you'd guess in this particular set of circumstances, will quell your fears and help you make a good shot.

Remember: a high bunker that prevents you from seeing the surface of the green foreshortens the distance and makes the flagstick seem a lot closer to the top of the bunker than it is. From that one perspective, behind the ball, it looks as if you have an extremely difficult shot, an almost straight-up lob that has to land softly on a tiny sliver of green, with virtually no margin for error.

Call it an optical illusion or an outright deception courtesy of the golf course's designer because if you walk around the bunker for a side view, you'll likely be pleasantly surprised. What you'll find, more often than not, is a much larger stretch of green to work with than you could possibly have anticipated by just looking from behind your ball.

A shot that seemed so intimidating suddenly looks makable, all because you took half a minute to really *look* at the shot from a second point of view. Now you're able to say to yourself, "Well, I don't have to hit that shot nearly as perfectly as I thought I did. I've got plenty of landing area here."

A special, even extreme, case? Sure. But I use it to make a point about having to *look* before you can *see* your shot. Use your eyes as you walk up to your ball. And always make sure to factor in a side view of the shot before attempting it.

If believing that a shot is going to be difficult creates undesirable tension, then finding out that it isn't reduces that tension. Remember: "Set your mind at ease so your body can perform."

THINK BIG

Phil Mickelson can be downright scary. When he needs to make a high-trajectory pitch from close to the green, he takes what seems like an impossibly big swing, so big the people in the gallery on the other side of the green start looking like sitting ducks. But instead of taking off like a rocket, his ball floats up high, then drops softly to the green like a butterfly with sore feet.

Most of the pros have this shot, but none pull it off more consistently and spectacularly than Mickelson. His secret? He trusts his club, his feel, and his swing.

Faced with a short pitch, the average golfer typically makes too short a swing because he *doesn't* trust his club, his feel, or his swing. Instead, he overworks his hands trying to flip the ball up, often to disastrous result.

Think long and lazy. Mickelson makes a big swing, not a hard one. Yes, you need energy to get the ball airborne, but let the energy come from a long, easy swing, not a short, hard one.

When in doubt, take a rehearsal swing that's even longer than the one you think you'll need. That'll make it seem less scary when you swing for keeps.

THE LOFTED PUTTER

Your ball is off the green, beyond the fringe, sitting up pretty decently in light to medium-length rough—the kind of average lie you expect to find when your approach to a par four green comes up a little short. How do you play this shot?

Putt it. That's right, putt it. Only use a six iron instead of a putter. Think of your six iron as a lofted putter.

Take the same grip with your six iron as you do with your putter. Take the same stance. Take care that your hands are about the same distance from the ground as they are with your putter. Note that with the shaft more upright than it is on a six-iron shot the heel of the club comes up slightly. That's okay: this is a putter now, not a six iron. Eyes over the ball. Now take the same stroke as you do with your putter, which is the most repeatable stroke in golf because there are so few moving parts: arms and forearms, no hands or wrists. The ball comes up and out of the grass on a low trajectory, lands softly just on the green, and rolls toward the pin.

Nice putt.

Do I always use the six iron? Do I always use the putting stroke around the green? Is this all there is to it?

The answers are no, no, and no. But if you work on the lofted putter idea, you'll find that it's the basic principle underlying many greenside shots.

○ ○ ○

DRILL: LEFT ARM ONLY

If you're having trouble making crisp contact with your greenside chips, try hitting some shots with your Left Arm Only. (That's if you're right-handed. If you're a lefty, the drill is called Right Arm Only.) This encourages a pendulum-like stroke, discourages excessive involvement of the hands and wrists, creates a descending arc with minimal follow-through, inhibits the lifting motion that leads to skulled shots, and helps you develop feel for the *swinging* force of the club head as opposed to a *snapping* wrist action.

THE EYES HAVE IT

Want a quick check on whether your ball is in the right position in your stance for the shot you're getting ready to play? Just close one eye and look.

For a chip, you should be able to see the front of the ball with your left eye—that means the ball's back in your stance. If you only see the top of the ball, it's too far forward.

For a pitch, your left eye should be straight down on the top of the ball—that means the ball's in the center of your stance. If you're able to see the front of the ball, it's too far back.

DRILL: THE TOM WATSON CHALLENGE

One of the greatest shots in the history of golf occurred on the seventeenth hole at Pebble Beach in the final round of the 1982 U.S. Open. Tom Watson, tied for the lead with Jack Nicklaus, who had completed the seventeenth playing in the group in front of him, slightly pulled his tee shot, which came to rest in deep rough, pin high, to the left of a green that sloped severely away from him. Watson only had about ten feet of green to work with, and any shot that slid past the hole wasn't likely to stop for another ten to fifteen feet because of the firmness of the green and the severity of the down slope. Tom visualized the flagstick serving as a backstop, took a few rehearsal swings with his sand wedge, then stepped up and hit his shot quickly.

You've probably seen the result—goodness knows, it's been shown on TV as much as any other shot in golf. Watson dropped his sand wedge into the long grass, his ball popped out on a fairly high trajectory, hit on the green, rolled softly and straight right into the flagstick, and dropped to the bottom of the cup for a birdie, giving him a little breathing room. Tom went on to birdie the seventy-second hole to win the Open by two strokes over Nicklaus.

Lucky shot? Not really. Not considering that it was Tom Watson who made it and that he'd been practicing that shot for over twenty years.

Stan Thirsk, an instructor in the Nicklaus-Flick Golf School, is Tom Watson's longtime teacher. Stan remembers Tom practicing his short game when he was a ten-year-old at the Kansas City Country Club. Young Tom would drop half a dozen balls at the side of the green, then hit them on the green and make the putt, not quitting until he got up and down on *every* ball. Later, as he got older and better, he'd keep working until he'd holed out a certain number that he'd set as the day's target. Stan says sometimes Tom would be out there until it was so dark he couldn't see the flagstick.

So let's do a modified version of the Tom Watson Up-and-Down Drill.

Take a few balls and drop them at various points around the green—some just off the fringe, some in longer rough, at least one the other side of a bunker. You can do this around a practice green, of course, but late in the afternoon out on the course when it's deserted is even better. Chip or pitch each ball to the flagstick—and putt out. Finishing a hole helps ingrain an attitude of competing and playing golf. And having a goal makes practicing more fun.

Set a reasonable target score, based on your skill level, and don't go in until you make that number, the idea being to put some pressure on yourself to be creative in solving problems. Keep a running log of your scores so you can monitor how much you improve. Eventually, of course, your target will be par: two shots per ball, just like the young Tom Watson.

THE DANGER OF TOO MUCH TV

If there's one shot the tour guys make that intrigues the average golfer more than a 300-yard drive, it's the one from 90 to 130 yards out that takes off as if it's going to fly the green, hits well past the pin, and spins back for a tap-in birdie. Looks like magic. Looks as if he had the ball on a string. Looks like something the guy sitting on his couch needs to learn how to do.

Bad idea.

Trying to hit that shot sets the average golfer up for defeat. He's not going to be able to create a lot of backspin unless he's playing a ball manufactured to deliver a lot of spin, which most golfers shouldn't be playing, and unless he devotes as much time to practice as the pros do. Moreover, what you can't tell from TV shots is that when a pro gets a lot of backspin, he's usually firing at an extremely firm green that's tilted toward him. For the vast majority of golfers, creating the proper trajectory makes much more sense than trying to create spin. Trajectory is a more consistent aid in stopping your ball than spin.

The goal, remember, is to land the ball softly and have it stop close to where it lands. Leave spin to politicians and pros.

EVERYBODY'S GOT AN ANGLE

When you're playing short pitch shots, you need to have a feel for the angle on which your club makes contact with the ball.

From a tight lie in short grass, you want to deliver the club head from an angle slightly inside the target line to add loft and get maximum elevation. To do this, you need a slightly open stance, the ball in the center of your stance, a slightly open club face, and a sweeping, pendulum-like stroke from the inside to get the ball up in the air.

From a deep lie in long grass, you need a sharp, descending angle to minimize interference from the grass lying behind the ball. To do this, you need your weight on your left leg and foot, a slightly open stance, the ball in the center of your stance, an open club face, and a descending (rather than sweeping) outside-in stroke to get the ball up in the air.

Both shots need to be played primarily with your arms and hands instead of your shoulders and your body. The feet and legs provide support. Both should feel like all arms—in other words, no wrist snapping, please. The shoulders and the body simply don't have the sensitivity to control the angle and the speed of the golf club on short-game shots. Without sensitivity to where the club head is and what it's doing, you're going to be lost around the green—and around the green is where the average golfer has the most room for improvement.

THE TEACHING GAP

Golf teachers, including yours truly, have not inspired people enough to understand and appreciate the importance of the short game. This is one case where emulating the tour players is absolutely the right thing to do, as most of them spend *more than half* their practice time on part shots (or, as we now know

SCORECARD SUMMARY

- Key Concept: *Low Shot = Low Risk, High Shot = High Risk.*
- The Basic Chip (Low Trajectory)
  1. Select club that delivers just enough height to carry ball onto green about three feet beyond collar.
  2. Ball toward back of stance, just to right of sternum.
  3. Hands just ahead of ball at address *and* at impact. Grip pressure slightly tighter than normal.
  4. Weight on left leg and foot.
  5. Left eye sees front of ball at address.
  6. Pendulum stroke. Arms and shoulders only; hands and wrists only react to weight of club head.
  7. Strike ball with descending arc.
  8. Don't be concerned with amount of follow-through. Club will generally run into ground.
- The Basic Pitch (High Trajectory)
  1. Select club that will deliver enough height so that the ball arrives at the desired landing spot in a steeply descending trajectory.
  2. Ball in middle of stance, under sternum.
  3. Hands even with ball at address and at impact.
  4. Weight evenly distributed.
  5. Right eye sees back of ball at address, left eye sees top of ball.
  6. Pendulum stroke. Mainly arms, shoulders respond. Allow whatever minimal wrist cock results from length of swing and weight in club head.
  7. Strike ball at bottom of swing arc.
  8. Don't be concerned with amount of follow-through. Momentum will take care of it.
- Golf is about scoring: short-game shots are scoring shots.

them, money shots), chips and pitches, bunker shots, and putting.

A good short game takes a huge amount of pressure off your full swing. If you can trust your ability to get up and down, you don't have to be perfect off the tee or with your long irons from the fairway. If your short game and your putter are working, you can always get back into the hole, even if you're not sure where your tee ball is going to wind up. And it's a whole lot easier to cut strokes off your score by sharpening your short game than by trying to get twenty more yards from your drive.

LESSON 11

A DAY AT THE BEACH

THE BEST BUNKER PLAYER I have ever seen is Corey Pavin. And I realized it when I watched him at the Ryder Cup in Oak Hills in 1995. Up until that time I would have said that the best bunker player was a toss-up between Gary Player, Bob Toski, Sam Snead, and Julius Boros. But Corey Pavin, I now believe, may well top them all.

On the eighteenth hole during the Thursday practice round, Corey's ball wound up in the bunker about forty-five feet from the hole. It was sitting up pretty nice in the sand because he'd rolled it in there with a long iron. So Corey walks into the trap—and I'd already watched him hole a bunker shot the day before and another that same day in the practice round—makes an easy practice swing, and hits a shot that lands softly, rolls across the green, straight at the pin, catches the top edge of the hole, and stops about two feet past.

The gallery has been joking with the golfers all day long, and now a voice pipes up, "Lucky."

Corey looks around, smiles, and says, "I don't think so."

Then he takes another ball out of his pocket and drops it in the sand. He doesn't even bother to set up, just takes another quick swing.

Well, the ball hits in almost exactly the same spot as the first one, rolls toward the pin, hits the bottom edge of the hole, and stops three inches away.

And Corey turns back to the guy who'd kidded him, grins again, and says, "I don't think so."

THE MOST FORGIVING SHOT IN GOLF

The average golfer had rather walk into a snake pit than into a bunker. The average pro had rather be in the sand than in the rough around it. Moral? Playing out of the sand doesn't have to be scary.

In fact, the bunker shot is the most forgiving shot in golf because it's the only one in which you don't have to hit the ball.

But just because the bunker shot is unique in that regard does not mean that you have to learn an entirely new golf swing. Indeed, for most golfers, I believe that the extreme outside-in swing that has been the standard for bunker play for many years is just dead wrong.

I don't believe the average golfer has enough time to devote to his game to fine-tune an entirely different swing for a shot he might need three or four times a round. So I teach the bunker shot like every other shot in golf. Swing the club for sand shots on basically the same arc as for other full-swing shots.

The fact is, many tour players today have started playing bunker shots based on their regular swing because they want the ball to come out of the sand and roll end over end when it hits the green, as if it had been putted. If they cut across it with an extreme outside-in swing, they get too much side spin and experience greater difficulty in controlling the golf ball. They will still have a variety of sand shots in their repertoire—they have to; golf is how they make their living—but I expect this evolution toward the regular swing for bunker play to continue.

So the good news about bunker shots—at least the way I teach them to most golfers—is that your point of origin is going to be your regular golf swing. The two swings aren't identical because we have to implement some adjustments to make the club face pass underneath the bottom of the ball without touching it. But I hope it takes a little of the terror out of bunker play to know that you won't have to learn an entirely new golf swing just to get off the beach.

I want to give you a simple, basic formula for getting Out, which has to be the average golfer's first goal. Out and On becomes the next goal. Later, if you have the time to practice and the right ideas to practice, the goal becomes Out, On, and Close.

But first comes Out.

THREE DEFINITIONS . . .

As precision instruments go, the sand wedge is not as complicated as, say, a surgical laser, but you do need to understand a few technical terms to use it properly.

The first and most obvious is the *face*, which is the part of the sand wedge that would, anywhere else on the course besides the bunker, be the only part of the club that makes contact with the ball. At address the face may be *open* (looking at the sky), *square* (perpendicular to the target line), or *closed* (staring just to the left of the target line).

Next is the *leading edge*, which is also pretty obvious—it's the front edge of the sand wedge, and it's what does all the damage when an incorrect swing produces direct contact with the ball instead of the sand. (You know, a skull shot out of the trap, over the green, and into the bushes by the next tee.) The leading edge does a lot of good, too, but in bunker play it must be employed cautiously.

Finally, and especially critical when you are trying to get out of the sand, is the *bounce.* This is the rounded bottom of the sand wedge that protrudes (in varying degrees) about an inch behind the leading edge. Strictly speaking, the bounce is merely another word for *bottom,* which means that all your

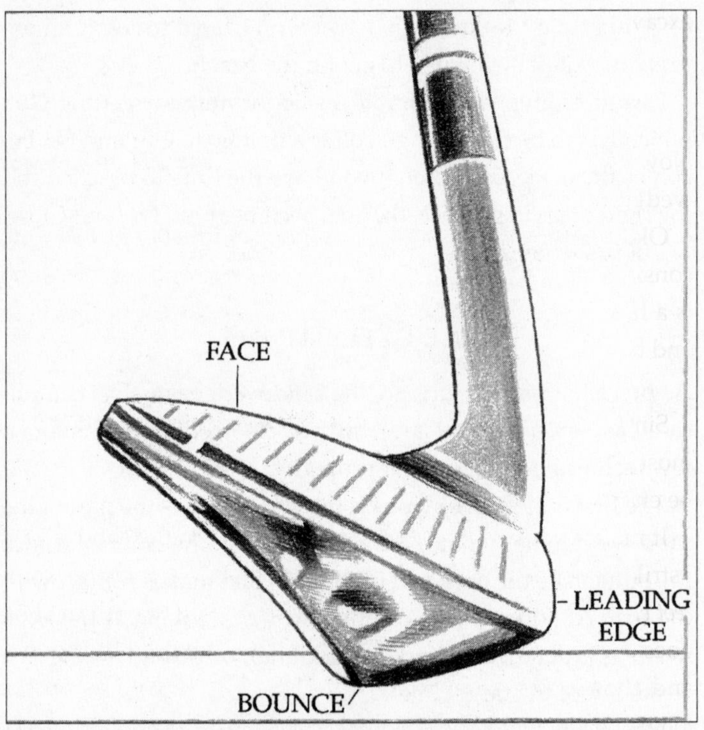

Know Your Instrument. And remember: when playing a shot from a bunker around the green, nothing you see here should ever touch the ball.

irons have one. But the bounce on the sand wedge—whether it is *deep* or *shallow*—is greater than the bounce on any other club in your bag. If it isn't, and obviously so, you need to get a new sand wedge.

The reason the bounce is so important is that, on all sand shots from average to good lies, it is the part of your club that makes primary contact with the sand. The bounce is what permits your club to slide through the sand and propel the sand and ball forward. If the instrument you use does not have an adequate bounce, and if you do not use that bounce properly, then you won't really be executing the bunker shot. You'll be excavating the bunker.

. . . AND ONE LAW OF PHYSICS

Now that we've mastered the engineering aspects of the sand wedge, let's turn to the laws of physics.

Okay, maybe it's not physics, which is probably just as well, considering how much I remember about the subject. But there is a law pertaining to bunker play that you must understand and believe in, and it is this:

The Ball Goes Where the Sand Goes.

Simple, huh? Probably too simple to be physics. But it's almost as fundamental as gravity. And if I had my way, it would be engraved on the face of every sand wedge.

It makes perfect sense. If my ball's sitting in the sand, and if I strike the sand behind it with my golf club, *and if there is no direct club-ball contact*, then the ball is going to go where the sand goes. How *far* it goes will depend on how I've used the bounce and the leading edge of my sand wedge, as well as on the length of my swing and the angle of my club head's descent. But the *direction* my ball takes depends almost entirely on only one thing: the direction the sand takes.

The reason I stress this—and students in the Nicklaus-Flick Golf School hear it over and over—is that, in the basic bunker shot, with your ball sitting up in the sand, I have to convince you that what your eyes are telling you is wrong.

I ask you to open your club face so you'll be able to make proper use of the bounce. ("Way open. More open than that. *Really* open. Right, that's good.") Now, you take one look at that club face open way to the right of the target, and your eyes tell you that your ball has to go where the face is looking. True, *but only if your club makes direct contact with the ball.*

Remember—and if you don't, I'll be sure to remind you—because there is no club-ball contact in greenside bunker shots, *the ball goes where the sand goes, not where the club face is looking.*

SAFETY FIRST

Sounds simple enough: no contact between club face and ball—none—and *not* hitting something ought to be easier than hitting it, right? Right, but just to make sure, here are the Six Sand Safety Rules that create the right conditions for *not* hitting the ball when getting it out of the sand and onto the green.

Sand Safety Rule 1. Adjust your club face to fit the lie, then take your grip—in that order. With a good lie in a greenside bunker, you want an open club face so that the bounce of your sand wedge will enter the sand first and slide under your ball, pushing it out, up, and on. The *only* way to make sure this happens consistently is to open the face of your club.

Sand Safety Rule 2. At address, lower your feet into the sand, toes first. This gets your body a little lower and drops the arc of your swing. Be sure to do the digging with your toes because that gets your weight on the balls of your feet and your upper body tilted out. This posture encourages an up-and-down swing arc, which helps you slide your club face under your ball. If you dig in and sit back on your heels, then the stroke tends to get too flat and has to come too much around your body.

Sand Safety Rule 3. Lean slightly to the left—far enough so that your eyes see the front of the ball. This helps ensure a descending swing.

Sand Safety Rule 4. Make sure the ball is in the center of your stance under your sternum. This is especially important in guarding against club-ball contact. If you play the ball forward, the club will bottom out too far behind the ball and you run the risk of clipping the ball on the upswing. If you want the club face to slide *under* the ball, then the arc of your swing should bottom out under the ball.

Sand Safety Rule 5. For an average lie, make sure your hands are slightly behind the ball at address. For a buried lie, you want your hands in front of the ball, putting the leading edge in the prevalent position, because you need to dig the ball out. But if most of the ball is above the sand, hands in front will cause you to drive the club too deep into the sand under the ball. Whatever you do, don't try to lift the club up at the bottom of your swing to help the ball; allow the sand to do its job, which is to push the ball out.

Sand Safety Rule 6. Stand tall, using the same posture as for your regular swing, bent at hips with knees only slightly flexed. You want to provide enough room for your arms to be able to swing downward rather than around so that the club head has a better chance of passing through the sand and underneath the ball. The average golfer sets up with too much bend in his knees. This leads him to lift the club and flip the ball out of the sand because his knees straighten out and force his body upward as the club swings downward—and those two forces are incompatible.

Now, since you've observed all the Sand Safety Rules, the next part is easy—just swing the club.

ALWAYS KNOW WHAT TIME IT IS

For most golfers, I teach a minimum ten o'clock arm swing. That's right, a minimum ten o'clock arm swing. I want the arms to get back past waist high to about ten o'clock—in other words, a big swing.

One perfectly natural reaction—I can see it on students' faces when I first tell them this, even if they don't say it—is "Hey, wait a minute. I only want to hit my ball fifteen yards. And he's saying swing my arms back to ten o'clock? Somebody's spent too many years out in the sun."

That's when I remind them that they're not trying to hit their *ball* fifteen yards. They're trying to hit about a large cupful of *sand* out of the trap.

Because there's no contact between the club head and the ball and because the sand is going to slow down the club head as it passes through it, you need a relatively long, slow swing to move the ball a relatively short distance.

More important, if your swing gets too short, your mind recognizes that you need more velocity to keep from stalling in the sand, and it sends out an all-points bulletin to swing faster and harder. Your grip pressure changes abruptly in response to this emergency signal, and either you pull the leading edge of your club into the ball, skulling it, or you drive the leading edge into the sand, where it comes to a screeching halt.

Sound familiar? It won't if you swing your arms back to ten o'clock high. (Note that I said "arms," not "club head," here.

Ten O'Clock and All's Well. Swinging your arms to ten o'clock offers your best hope for escape from the desert.

Your arms point to ten o'clock. Your club head will be in another time zone and you won't be able to see it without corkscrewing your neck.)

For the average golfer, the most effective greenside bunker swing is going to feel like lots of arms, long and slow. Now, it's true that many pros, when they're trying to put spin on the ball, use a much shorter, much more aggressive swing. Remember, their goal is not just to get Out and On but to get Out, On, and Close—or *in*. If I want spin on my ball, then I've got to have a shorter, aggressive arc to quickly knock the sand out from underneath the ball. But I've got to spend many hours learning to play that shot. If I don't have that kind of time, I'd rather play a shot that fits my regular golf swing.

For most golfers in a greenside bunker, a pendulum arc generated by a minimum ten o'clock arm swing offers the best, most repeatable way *out*.

HOW FAR BEHIND THE BALL?

You may have noted that none of the Sand Safety Rules talks about how far behind the ball the club head should make contact with the sand. The reason is that for the average golfer who follows the method outlined above, it doesn't really matter that much.

That may sound heretical, but I think most people try to be far too precise about the contact point with the sand in bunker shots. If you're trying to calibrate exactly three or four inches or whatever behind the ball as your point of entry, it's going to cause tension, and tension will tie you up.

If you have a long enough swing (at least to ten o'clock!), if you use the bounce properly, and if the face of your club passes underneath the ball, then making contact with the sand anywhere from two to five inches behind your ball will get it out and on the green.

HOW MUCH SAND?

"A cupful" is my quick answer when a student asks how much sand he should stake on a bunker shot. But then that old kids' riddle flashes through my mind—How many balls of string would it take to reach the moon? One, if it were long enough—and I realize I need to be a little more precise.

Not a demitasse cupful.

Not a standard-size coffee cupful.

Not a measuring cupful.

The cupful you're looking for is enough sand to fill one of those large paper cups used in those fancy coffee bars that seem to be popping up everywhere.

(Bonus tip: until you build up your confidence in bunker play, stick with the decaf.)

TEN CUPS

If I were to ask you to hit ten straight balls out of a sand trap and onto the green, what would your reaction be? My guess is that if you're an average golfer, you'd think that was a pretty tough assignment.

But what if I asked you to hit ten large cupfuls of sand, one at a time, onto the green? Well, let me tell you something—they're one and the same thing.

Charley Epps, a senior instructor at the Nicklaus-Flick Golf School (and another of the faculty members who's on *Golf* magazine's Top 100 Teachers in America list), introduced the "Bunker Cocktail." This is not something you turn to in despair when you find yourself stranded on the beach. It's a large paper cupful of sand garnished with a golf ball that, I explain to students, has to be removed from the trap. One look at the Bunker Cocktail helps you visualize just how much sand you have to move to get your ball out, and that in turn helps you understand why you need such a big swing.

To get your *ball* out of a bunker, all you need to know is how to get *sand* out of a sand trap. You don't have to worry about the ball. The ball's just going along for the ride.

To make sure you're prepared for that assignment, grab your specially designed sand removal instrument (your sand wedge), hop into the nearest bunker, and practice hitting bunker shots—*without* a ball. That's right, just practice hitting sand out of the bunker, making sure to follow all the Sand Safety Rules. Doesn't sound so scary if you think of it that way, does it? In fact, what could be easier?

GOOD LIES, BAD LIES, DAMN LIES

As with every other shot in golf, the first thing you do with a bunker shot is inspect the lie. As always, this is critically important because how your ball's sitting is going to determine how you use your instrument to get it out of the sand and onto the green. Do you use the bounce to *slide* the club face under the ball? Or do you use the leading edge to *dig* into the sand under the ball? Depends on the lie.

It may not seem like it, but most of the time you'll have a good lie. Think about it. Your approach comes in a little hot, runs through the green, skips into the bunker, and rolls dead a couple of inches ahead of its crater—on top of the sand. Or a lofted shot comes up just short, hits the side of the green, rolls back into the trap, and comes to rest—on top of the sand. Sure, you're occasionally going to mis-hit a short pitch that drops straight down, hard enough to create a crater but not hard enough to bounce out of it. But more often than not, you can expect an average-to-good lie.

For a *good lie,* you want to use the bounce of the club to keep the leading edge from digging in too much. Just remember: Safety First and Ten O'Clock High. You open the face, and you knock a large cupful of sand onto the green.

But let's say you have a *bad lie.* Your ball hit hard and didn't bounce out of its crater: the infamous fried-egg lie. Or somebody neglected to rake the bunker and your ball ends up in a deep furrow. You visualize your stroke carrying the club face underneath that ball, and you realize that the cut of sand displaced by the bounce of your sand wedge isn't going to be deep enough. So now you've got to change the way the club enters the sand by adjusting the leading edge. Put the ball in the center of your stance, as you would for a normal sand shot, but lean a little more left, which will make you swing down in a steeper arc. Now square the face to slightly closed so the club will dig rather than slide. Then swing the club so that the leading edge enters the sand at the outer edge of the fried egg—or about two inches behind the ball in the furrow—and slices underneath the bottom of the ball.

Sometimes, though, you are going to be the victim of what can charitably be described as a *damn lie.* Your ball rolls up against the front lip of a steep trap, preventing you from following through on your swing. Or your ball trickles into an edge of the bunker so that you have to stand outside and swing down on a target that's a foot below your feet. Or, when watering the green that morning, the groundsmen let the sprinkler soak the bunker as well, and your ball ends up in a swamp.

Then, nightmare of nightmares, there's the worst damn lie of all, the one that makes you realize, once and forever, that the Golf Gods are not only all-powerful but also capricious and possessed of a mighty peculiar sense of humor. I'm talking about the lie that results when you hit an almost perfect approach shot—the key word here is "almost"—that, instead of hitting on a grassy mound just beyond the bunker and rolling up to three feet, nose-dives hard into the steep face of the bunker and buries deep in the wet sand, leaving only about ten dimples showing. The dreaded *plug*.

The plug offers the supreme challenge to your belief—your faith—that the ball goes where the sand goes. Why? Because I'm going to ask you to turn the toe of the club inward, creating a severely closed face. Then, with a steeply descending blow, use the club like a hoe to dig your ball out. The toe of the club digs around and under the ball, compressing the sand forcefully and causing the ball to pop out. For a really severe plug, it's the only way.

The moral here is that there are ways to get out of even the worst damn lies. They involve plenty of imagination, the creative use of your club's leading edge and bounce—and sometimes even its toe—and some experience (and practice!) handling ordinary good lies and merely bad lies.

Oh, and one more thing: it wouldn't hurt to make your peace with the Golf Gods. That means you never say, after a good shot that earns "oohs" and "ahs" from your playing partners, that you finally "have it." If you do, whatever it is you think you "have" you're sure to lose within a couple of holes. The Golf Gods do *not* like to be trifled with.

○ ○ ○

The Good . . . For a shot from a good lie on top of the sand, open the club face.

The Bad . . . For a shot from a not-so-good lie sitting down in the sand, square the club face.

The Ugly . . . For a shot from a horrible lie half-buried in the sand, close the club face.

THE LEFT FOOT, RIGHT TOE, RIGHT-HAND-OFF-AFTER-IMPACT DRILL

This drill is a lot harder to say three times in rapid succession than it is to do. And I don't know of any other single drill that is better for building good bunker habits.

1. Set up the usual way with the ball in the middle of your stance, dig your toes into the sand, and open your club face.
2. Now, put all your weight on your left foot, and lift your right foot so that your toe is just touching the sand where your heel had been to help keep you balanced.
3. Take a full, slow, arms-back-to-ten-o'clock backswing, just as you would in a normal sand shot.
4. To help maintain your spine angle through the shot, release the grip with your right hand after impact and complete the swing with your left arm folding softly.

Most bad bunker shots are the result of one of two things. Either the left side of the body lifts up, which causes the leading edge of the club face to skull the ball out of the trap, across the green, and into the trap on the other side. Or the right hand takes charge, twists the club face, and drives the leading edge into the sand, which causes the ball to hop a couple of inches and die.

What the Left Foot, Right Toe, Right-Hand-Off-After-Impact Drill does is train you to maintain your spine angle through the swing and keep your body from pulling up at the last second. This drill also helps you develop a feel for the descending blow that you want in a bunker shot. And it teaches you that you can finish your shot without having your right hand taking charge to "help" things along. Finally, this drill helps instill rhythm and balance in your swing. If you lurch up while standing on one leg, for instance, you're likely to fall on your butt.

You probably won't be surprised to learn that Left Foot, Right Toe, Right-Hand-Off-After-Impact is not only great for bunker shots but for your full swing and part shots as well.

But you may be surprised to hear that this is one drill that I *do* recommend that golfers who are working on their bunker game take with them onto the Playing Ground. If you're a little bit anxious about your bunker play, take a long rehearsal swing—longer than you think you'll need—and then use Right-Hand-Off-After-Impact when you make your actual shot.

There's no telling what a few up-and-outs will do for your confidence level.

LONG SHOT

Long bunker shots from around the green are governed by the same Sand Safety Rules, the same swing (arms to minimum ten o'clock), and the same ironclad "Thou Shalt Not Have Club-Ball Contact" principle that apply to close-in greenside bunkers. And yes, the ball still goes where the sand goes.

What's different is your instrument. Take a pitching wedge, a nine iron, even an eight: the less-lofted club will give you more distance with no change in effort. Open the club face slightly to expose the bounce. Standard bunker setup, standard bunker swing.

Doesn't that sound easier than trying to horse your ball thirty yards with a prodigious, full-bore, take-no-prisoners slash with your sand wedge? Believe me, it is—and a *lot* safer.

○ ○ ○

FAIRWAY BUNKERS

Your first order of business in a fairway bunker—after inspecting your lie, of course—is to check your escape route. Too many people worry about the distance to the green when they should first be certain of selecting a club that will clear the lip of the bunker. Priority number one, after all, is getting out.

That means, if you catch a bad lie or the lip of the bunker is too severe, you may have to take your medicine—that is, take a lofted club and *just get out*.

But if you have a good to average lie, and if you have a decent escape route (e.g., the lip of the bunker is not too high), you have every right to more ambitious goals.

Step one is to take at least one extra club: if the distance is a six iron, use a five, perhaps even a four. Play the ball slightly back in your stance. Scrunch your toes into the sand a little for stability. For better contact and to offset your feet digging into the sand, grip down on the club. (Notice that I said "grip" down, not "choke" down. Mr. Penick used to say, "Never use the word 'choke' around a golfer.") Take a three-quarter-length swing for control. Make sure your swing is mostly arms and hands; your body and legs should be very quiet.

The point of all this emphasis on control and measured movement is that in the fairway bunker shot there *is* club-ball contact—and it needs to be precise to be successful. Remember the marvelous bunker shot that Sandy Lyle made at the eighteenth at Augusta to win the 1988 Masters? He couldn't have made a neater cut with a scalpel.

Your goal: hit the little ball before you hit the big ball.

○ ○ ○

THREE-IN-ONE

In a bunker with a low to medium lip, line up three balls along the target line, each ball close to but not quite touching the next. Want to bet I can't knock all three on the green with one shot?

Don't take that bet.

I do this three-in-one shot for students at the Nicklaus-Flick Golf School to drive home a single, simple point about bunker play: if you follow the Sand Safety Rules, as described above, you don't even have to hit a precise distance behind the ball to get it out of the trap and onto the green.

As with all bunker shots, what gets each ball up and out in the three-in-one shot is the force of the sand moving against it, with the sand in turn being moved by the club head. What I'm looking for in the three-in-one is a stroke that makes the cut of sand stay pretty constant for a long period of time.

The first ball comes out fairly high because the club head is moving rapidly through the sand and pushing it forward and up. The second ball comes out a little lower because the club head is slowing down. And the third ball barely carries out over the lip of the trap but rolls a long way. But all three come out, and they end up about ten feet apart—on the green.

What does that show you? Well, it shows that you don't have to be as perfect as you might think. You may not hit the marvelous-looking sand shots that the tour guys do, you won't become as adept at playing out of every type of sand, and you won't hole out as many or get up and down as often.

But you *can* play bunker shots reasonably well—get out and onto the green and give yourself a chance to save par. Always start by visualizing the club face passing underneath the bottom of the ball, regardless of the lie. Then follow the Sand Safety Rules, make your regular golf swing, and make sure you avoid making contact with your ball. That way, like Corey Pavin, you won't have to depend on luck to get off the beach.

SCORECARD SUMMARY

- To avoid club-ball contact and to put you in the best position to get *out* of the sand, be sure to play by the Sand Safety Rules.
  1. Adjust club face to fit lie—open for average lies—*then* take grip.
  2. Lower feet into sand, toes first.
  3. Lean slightly left to encourage a descending blow.
  4. Play ball in center of your stance.
  5. Hands slightly behind ball at address (for average lies) to ensure that bounce of club makes initial contact with sand.
  6. Stand tall, bent at hips, with knees only slightly flexed—same as for any other full-swing shot.
  7. Take a long, slow-feeling swing—arms to minimum ten o'clock—and splash about a large cup of sand onto the green, *with no club-ball contact.*
- Use bounce of club to make club face pass under the ball.
- Key Concept: *The ball goes where the sand goes.*

LESSON 12

THE OTHER 50 PERCENT OF THE GAME

NOTHING IN GOLF IS more personal or more idiosyncratic than putting. There are almost as many putting styles as there are golfers—and the most recent count by the National Golf Foundation sets the number of "avid" golfers in the United States (i.e., golfers who play more than twenty rounds a year) at 15.7 million.

But that's nothing compared to the number of different sizes, shapes, and kinds of putters there are out there. Blade putters, mallet putters, you-name-it putters. Short, regular, long, and superlong putters. Golfers have given their putters nicknames—"Calamity Jane" (Bobby Jones), "Little Ben" (Ben Crenshaw), "Unprintable" (most of the rest of us).

It's hard to overemphasize the importance of the putter, not when a golfer uses it for half his shots. No other club can match it for the emotional devastation wrought by a three-footer missed, no other can provide the emotional lift of a twenty-footer drained.

Yet unless you count rolling a dozen putts five minutes before your tee time "practicing"—and I don't—it's fair to say that the average golfer barely practices putting at all. And when he does find himself spending more time than usual on the practice green—say, when there's a backup on the first tee—he doesn't really have a concept to guide him.

No wonder he consistently gives away a ton of strokes on the green.

Granted, as axioms go, "Drive for Show, Putt for Dough" may not be as true as it once was. Older courses with more traditional layouts tend to be more forgiving off the tee, less punitive when shots stray from the fairway. Most of the trouble at a Donald Ross course, for instance, is found around and on the greens. Newer courses tend to make life more difficult off the tee—on many, the punishment for an errant tee shot is worse than for armed robbery. With fewer chances of recovery if you hit one sideways, there's a greater premium on accuracy with your driver.

Even so, *half* the strokes needed to shoot even par on any course, old or new, are intended to be made with the putter.

Half, as in 50 percent.

So tell me, do you spend 50 percent of your practice time working on your putting?

THE SIX COMPONENTS OF PUTTING

Putting is more art than science, and much more about feel than mechanics. Even so, a good place to begin is by analyzing putting's six essential components.

1. Reading the Green. Right to left? Left to right? Straight in? Uphill? Downhill? Slow? Fast? Against the grain? With the grain? A lot of questions, and you won't find the answers to them on the driving range hitting your driver. Learning to read greens comes only with experience, not to mention a whole lot of trial and error. The best way is to go for the big picture—and I mean that literally. After analyzing the specific conditions that will affect your ball's movement over the green's surface, create in your mind a complete moving picture of your ball rolling across the green and into the cup. That picture should include the ball's initial velocity when it leaves your putter face, the turn it makes in response to the green's contours, and the last few feet, when it begins to slow down in preparation for rolling over the lip and into the bottom of the cup. Oh, and be sure to add one sound effect: Plonk!

2. *Aim.* Okay, you've read the green and come up with answers to all those questions. Now it's time to translate them into a target line—and stick with it. The ultimate target, of course, is the hole, but for most putts, and especially for longer ones, it helps to have a couple of intermediate targets along the way—a blemish in the grass, a speck of dirt, a (repaired!) ball mark—that you *know* you can hit. Aim your putter's face dead square to your target line.

3. *Speed Control.* I believe you should have one—and only one—speed producer in putting. For the average golfer, whose lifestyle permits only a limited amount of playing and practicing, that speed producer should be the arms, not the hands and wrists.

4. *Squaring the Putter Face at Impact.* Where your putter is facing at impact has more influence on where the putt goes than your swing path. Good putters feel the exact position of their putter face throughout the putting stroke. Nobody who's ever played the game has been better from ten feet in as Jack Nicklaus, and nobody's ever been a better putter on fast greens. The key to his putting success, Jack says, is his ability to use the putter to make square contact.

5. *Repeating Stroke.* As in the full swing, a repeating stroke in putting evolves from good habits. Stable and relaxed posture, body bent at hips, allowing room for your arms to hang from your shoulder sockets and swing freely. Eyes directly over the ball. Secure grip and striking the ball in the exact center of the putter face. Nerves are the most common cause of disruption of the putting stroke: you're putting for a par and the right to have somebody else pick up the tab at the nineteenth hole, and suddenly a four-foot straight-in putt changes into a twenty-five-foot snake, right before your eyes. This is where you'll be happy you have a putting stroke with one speed producer—the arms—because it's the most likely to repeat.

6. *Attitude.* Putting is so much about confidence. A good putter *believes* he's a good putter. He *loves* his putter. He *loves* to putt. Conversely, if you *don't* believe you're a good putter, you won't be. Also, you probably won't spend the time to develop good habits if you don't like to putt—in which case, improvement in your putting will hinge on an attitude adjustment.

THE PUTT AND THE PENDULUM

Speed control starts with being able to *feel* the swinging force of the putter's head against the back of the ball. I believe the best way to do that is with a pendulum-like stroke: I think your images and your chance of being consistent are much better if you're thinking "pendulum" rather than "hit" or "accelerate."

As the single most important component of putting is speed, I feel strongly that there should be just one source of speed in your putting stroke. More than that and you're asking for big trouble.

There is the Hands-Wrists School, in which you lock your arms to your sides and generate putter speed with your hands and wrists. Arnold Palmer and Billy Casper are deans of this school.

Then there is the Arms-Shoulders School, which calls for no wrist action at all, with your arms and shoulders providing all the impetus. Tom Watson and Bob Charles are honor-roll students in the Arms-Shoulders School. Most of the players on the PGA Tour and the LPGA Tour are Arms-Shoulders putters.

Finally, there is the Ben Crenshaw School. Ben uses a combination of arms, hands, and wrists that is unique to him. Well, a few others have tried it, but none has come close to achieving his success.

(And by the way, don't believe for a minute that Ben's brilliant putting has all that much to do with his famous "Little Ben" putter. The secret to his putting is his amazing sensitivity and his confidence, not his putter. Ben Crenshaw would be a great putter with a hockey stick.)

The worst putters generally have two things in common—a putting stroke that (1) fails to deliver the putter face squarely to the ball and (2) produces erratic speed control. In other words, they're flunk-outs of the Crenshaw School. They use their arms and shoulders to bring the putter back, then flip their wrists at impact. Anytime you have two speed producers, you have too many things that can go wrong.

A lot of good putters—maybe a majority of the very best—have been Hands-Wrists putters. But they are professionals who putt every day, and they have developed extraordinary feel in their hands.

For the average golfer, whose lifestyle doesn't permit daily practice on a putting green, I recommend a putting stroke controlled by the arms and shoulders, with quiet hands and wrists. This is the best way for most golfers to control speed. Active hands produce too many variations of speed at impact, particularly in a tight match when nerves kick in.

As a footnote, the surging appeal of the long putter—many pros, young and old, here and in Europe, are turning to it—is based in large measure on its contribution to speed control. Because one end is wedged against the body, controlling speed is simplified. Dave Pelz, one of the premier students of the short game, argues that the long putter affords the best chance of making a pendulum-like stroke.

The long putter has also proved beneficial to some golfers who suffer from the yips. The stability of the long shaft held against the body tends to diminish the havoc caused by twitchy hands. I prefer the Bernhard Langer stroke for those prone to occasional attacks of the yips—that is, a standard-length putter but one with the shaft clamped against the left wrist and lower forearm by the right hand, effectively making the putter an extension of the left arm and taking the wrists out of play.

The cross-handed grip—left hand below right hand—also helps eliminate wristiness and build an Arms-Shoulders putting stroke. Indeed, for beginning golfers, and even for more experienced golfers willing to make a major-league time commitment to change, I recommend the cross-handed grip as the best way to control speed in putting.

THE TOP EIGHT REASONS NOT TO PRACTICE PUTTING

If David Letterman were a golfer, he'd undoubtedly come up with ten. But until he takes up the game, we'll just have to make do with the top eight reasons for not working on their putting I've heard from golfers over the years.

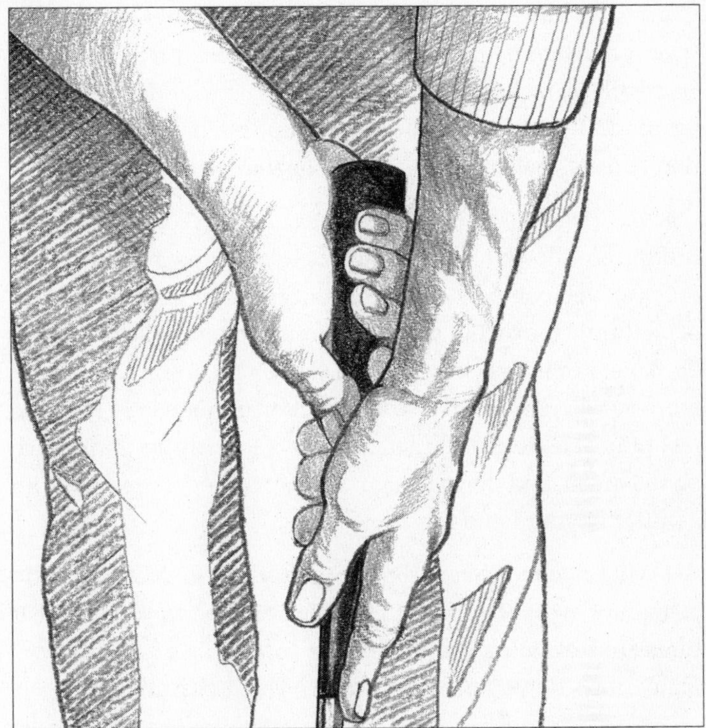

The Pendulum Grip. If I were starting from scratch in golf, this is the putting grip I'd use, because it encourages a pendulum-like putting stroke.

1. *Ben Hogan Didn't.* Yes, he did. Toward the end of his career Mr. Hogan clearly preferred hitting crisp three irons 205 yards to three feet than trying to negotiate the last thirty-six inches with his putter. And he's supposed to have said that he wished the game of golf did not include putting at all. But he practiced putting, you can be sure of it. Those four U.S. Open titles are proof of it. Sam Snead felt that at the height of his career Hogan was the best in the business from ten feet in.

2. *It's No Fun.* Compared to what? Three putts from inside twenty-five feet? An eight-footer for birdie that whimpers to a standstill six inches from the cup? An extra four or five strokes a round? If putting practice is no fun, it's only because you don't create challenges and use drills that make it fun.

3. *You Either Have the Touch or You Don't.* Not bad, as self-fulfilling philosophies go. And even better as a copout. Not only can you compensate in great measure for a supposed lack of "natural" touch, but you can tap and enhance the touch you do have. I'm not saying that Ben Crenshaw doesn't have a lot more sensitivity and feel with a putter in his hands than the rest of us. He does. But there are ways to increase your touch on the green, and they all begin with spending more time with a putter in your hands.

4. *My Long Irons Need Work.* Sure they do. So do mine. So do just about everybody's. But how many times do you pull that three iron of yours out of the bag in a typical round? How many times do you use your putter? The prosecution rests.

5. *The Practice Green Is Too Different from the Greens on the Course.* Maybe so, but so what? Yes, a lot of courses don't have the resources to maintain practice facilities as well as they might. And even at courses that do, no practice green can offer all the different contours and speeds you'll encounter on the golf course. But that doesn't mean you can't improve your putting by spending quality time on the practice green. By that logic, a singer would never bother learning musical notes because they are used differently in different songs.

6. *It Doesn't Seem to Matter.* Ah, the frustration excuse. You spend a solid, focused half hour on the practice green rolling every putt straight and true, only to go out on the course and

three-jerk on the first hole to start your day with a double bogey. Welcome to golf. Hadn't you noticed that it's "flog" spelled backward? It's the very nature of the game, and the essence of its strange appeal, that golf is able to reward, punish, surprise, and disappoint, as if it had a will of its own. Which it does. All I can say is that if you keep at it, if practicing putting becomes as integral to your golf game as lacing up your golf shoes, then it will, eventually, most definitely, matter.

7. It Hurts My Back. Anyone who has ever suffered from lower back pain—and medical people tell us that's about a third of the population at one time or another—knows that this is a legitimate excuse for not standing, partly bent over, torso immobilized, for long periods of time. Fuzzy Zoeller, who has suffered serious back trouble for a number of years, finds putting for any length of time an ordeal. Other tour players who suffer from lower back pain have the same trouble with putting practice, though not to the degree that Fuzzy does.

The key is *not* to spend your entire putting session hunched over in one position—and not just because it's better for your back.

If you throw down three or four balls, assume your putting position, and start putting, one putt after another, without altering your position, you're placing a lot of stress on your lower back—and you're not doing your putting game much good. If you're not walking around behind your ball, setting your target line, visualizing your ball rolling across the green into the hole, and *then* stepping up to putt, how much are you learning that is useful on the golf course? Stroking three or four balls without looking down the target line from behind and determining speed and break may help groove your stroke, but it's not going to do very much for your ability to put the ball in the cup when it counts—unless, of course, you play some funny game that allows you to use three balls when you reach the green.

You can alleviate stress on your lower back *and* do more for your putting if you have more frequent sessions of shorter duration—and if you stand up and move around between putts. Go through your normal Pre-Shot Routine with each practice putt. Your back will thank you. And so will your scorecard.

8. I Don't Have Time. Then go find some stimulating, fulfilling, challenging human endeavor that, unlike golf, does not require a commitment of time and effort to realize maximum enjoyment. And call me when you find it.

A CAUTIONARY TALE

Best known today as an astute TV commentator, Judy Rankin won twenty-eight tournaments on the LPGA Tour—and would have made it into the LPGA Hall of Fame if she had not tried to accelerate her putter as she brought it through the ball.

At least that's what Judy says now, looking back at a career that included seven losses in play-offs, four of them a result of three-putting.

The way Judy explains it, from time to time the backswing on her putting stroke tended to get too short. When it did, she would compensate with a quicker forward swing. The effort of trying to accelerate on her forward swing created a change in grip pressure, which in turn changed the speed and the face alignment of her putter at impact. She feels now that that concept—as opposed to a pendulum concept—really hurt her.

With most good putters, the forward swing is shorter than the backswing for the simple reason that the ball gets in the way, slowing down the pendulum-like stroke. I see that in Ben

Crenshaw. I see it in Jack Nicklaus. One major exception to the general rule is Paul Azinger, who has a very short backswing and clearly accelerates quickly through the ball.

Most golfers, though, are going to be more successful with a pendulum-like stroke. Ask Judy Rankin.

KEEP SCORE

Ask a guy who's played golf earlier in the day what he shot, and he tells you without giving it a second thought.

Ask the same guy how many putts he took, and chances are he'll put you on hold as he mentally replays the entire round.

The fact is, most golfers can't tell you within three how many putts they took without doing some quick mental math.

Next time you play, note on your scorecard the number of putts you take. Award yourself a par for every two-putt green, a birdie for one-putt efforts, and a bogey every time it takes you three putts to get the ball in the hole. (Even though official tour stats don't, please count shots from the fringe as putts if you use your putter.)

I think you'll be surprised at the number of putts you're actually taking—and at the extra strokes those three-putt (and worse!) greens add to your score.

Awareness is the first step to understanding. And understanding is a prerequisite for improvement. So log your putts.

POINT OF VIEW

You stroke a putt, and you watch the ball roll toward the hole. Fine—every golf shot deserves a sympathetic gallery. But where do you watch *from*?

To assist in the development of a repeating stroke, I believe you should watch your ball from the striking position. You need accurate feedback on what happened to the ball when you struck it—and you didn't strike it standing straight up.

When I raise up to watch my putt, my view isn't the same as when I was rotating my eyes along the target line prior to taking the putter back. The upright vantage point feeds slightly discordant information into my mind's computer about the relationship between my aim and stroke and my putt's direction and speed.

And that leads to what computer people used to call GIGO: Garbage In, Garbage Out.

THE RUNYAN DRILL

One of the best putting drills I know comes from Paul Runyan, who had one of the greatest short games of anybody who ever played the game of golf.

Get three balls and start with a straight three-foot putt on a flat part of the green. Try to make the first putt so that the ball just manages to drop over the front edge of the hole on its very last turn. Make the second ball go into the hole with enough speed to carry it all the way to the back liner. Give the third ball a Tom Watson slam-dunk-knock-it-to-the-back-of-the-hole so hard that it bounces up, then drops in.

Sounds simple—and from three or four feet, it is—but what you're doing is really pretty profound. What you're doing in this drill is making your stroke react to a picture. And *you're* calling the picture.

This is critical for attitude because when you say, "I'm going to make this putt *this* way," you're committing to something concrete. Not just a general "I'm going to make this putt" but "I'm going to make it *my* way."

Now, move back four feet and do the same things again. It's a little harder, sure, but it's teaching an important lesson.

You're not mechanically working on your putting stroke—you're letting the roll of the ball help you find it.

Next, find a place on the green where there's some contour. This is where it gets fun. You want to start out from close in—three feet, maybe two—and move back in small increments. And you want to move around the hole and putt from different spots so that you have to factor in all the breaks and make appropriate adjustments in speed and aim.

The point is that the clearer a picture you have of a putt, the more decisive you are in picking the stroke that matches the picture and thus the more committed you are to making the putt. That's what learning in golf is all about—experimenting to decide which solutions are best suited to your attitude.

This drill drives home one of the basic truths about putting: speed determines line. Let me repeat: *speed determines line.* Think about it. It makes sense to play your putt to break six inches only if your putting stroke produces the right speed to make that six-inch break work.

If you just stand on the green thinking about its contours without thinking about speed, you will never have a usable picture of the kind of putt you want to make.

On a putt that needs a lot of break, if you want to let the ball die in the hole, you take one routing. If you want to carry it to the center of the cup, another. And if you want to ram it into the back of the hole, well, maybe you take all the break out of the putt entirely. Whichever option you choose, you must visualize the putt going in before you even touch the ball. Make a commitment based on a picture that *you* create, then let your stroke react to your picture.

○ ○ ○

DO IT WITH YOUR EYES CLOSED

Put three balls on the green, side by side. Pick a target about five feet away—a spike mark, a leaf, a penny, whatever. Now assume your putting stance, look down at your ball, *close your eyes*—and putt.

Easy, wasn't it? Bet you surprised yourself at how close you came to your target.

Now do it again, only this time try to putt your second ball six inches past the first one. Then make the third go six inches past the second.

Once you've mastered the three-ball progression in the Eyes Closed Drill—did I mention that with each ball it becomes increasingly harder?—you're ready for the advanced version.

Same setup—three balls, eyes closed when you putt—only this time you call in advance ("six inches short," "six inches long") where each putt is going.

You might want to bring along a tape measure to keep yourself honest on this one. And to determine who won, in case you get into a little betting game with a friend. (It's amazing how pressure changes the equation.)

What this drill does, as I'm sure you've figured out by now, is help you develop feel and sensitivity for your putter. You'll find that you don't need your eyes to know whether you've struck the ball squarely.

The elements that produce a repeating stroke on the green—eyes over ball, relaxed posture, secure grip, arms relaxed—are basically mechanical.

But speed control—the most important single facet of putting—is a function of feel.

○ ○ ○

DRILL: FLAGSTICK TAP

A putt's no different from any other shot: if you don't make solid contact, if the sweet spot on the club face does not strike the ball squarely, if the club face is not perpendicular to the target line at impact, then the ball will not—can not—roll where you want it to.

You might figure, heck, on a short stroke like a putt, with no swing planes and shoulder turns and hip drives to mess me up, making square contact is a snap. Well, you'd be figuring wrong, and I can prove it.

Pull the flagstick out of the hole and lay it on the green. The stick is your target line, the flat-headed metal cylinder that fits in the hole is your ball. Assume your putting stance, aim down your target line, and give the "ball" your best stroke, the kind you use on those pesky eight-footers that, doggone it, you ought to be able to drop more than you do.

Thunk?

Or clank?

Your ears will tell you whether you're making square contact, that is, whether the sweet spot on your putter head runs into the end of the flagstick. So will your hands. You'll hear and feel even slightly off-center hits, as well as those glancing blows that set up three-putt greens—and worse.

(You don't need a flagstick to do this drill, of course. A foot-long piece of half-inch wooden dowel works equally well in helping you identify square hits and is a lot more portable. But Dowel Drill sounds too much like a carpentry term.)

The Flagstick Tap helps you learn to keep the putter face perpendicular to the target line for square, solid contact. And that's exactly the point where all good putts begin.

○ ○ ○

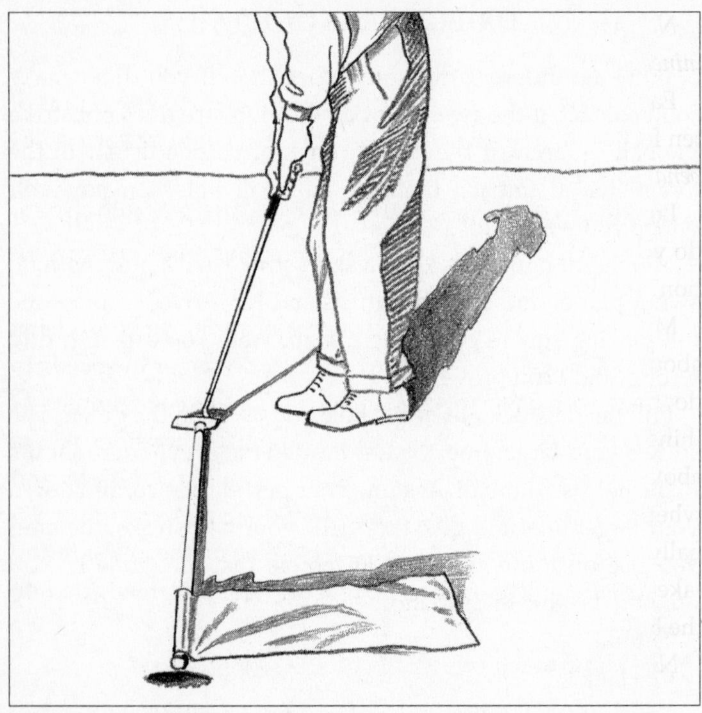

Thunk! The sound your putter makes when it whacks solidly against the butt end of a flagstick will tell you when you make square contact.

SPEED TRAP

Inside right edge?

Yes.

One ball outside?

Go for it.

Start it a foot to the right?

I like that.

Are you nuts? How can it be all three? I'm talking about the same putt.

No, you're not. Or have you already forgotten that speed determines line?

Each answer to your question about where to aim a putt of ten feet or more with some curvature to it could be correct, *depending on the speed.*

Looking to rap your ball firmly into the back of the cup? Or do you see it dying into the hole, dropping on its last revolution? Or somewhere in between?

My point here is that you can't make an informed decision about how much break to play unless you factor in speed. To do that, you have to take into consideration a number of things—the severity of the green's curvature, whether you're above or below the hole, the speed of the green itself, and whether the ball will be rolling with or against the grain. Finally, you need to walk halfway to the hole on the low side and take a mental picture of the ball rolling over the green and into the hole.

Now, how much break did you say that putt has?

DRILL: TEN-BALL PROGRESSION

On a green with some slope to it, line up eight to ten balls, the first six inches from the hole and the rest on out to a distance of fifteen to twenty feet, on a line that follows the curvature of the green. Beginning with the ball closest to the hole, knock each ball in—or try to—one after the other, with each ball tracking over the line of the previous one. Pay attention to the effect of increasing distance on the length of your stroke and on the relationship between speed and line.

As goofy as it looks, I even have my tour players step up to the ball and knock in that first one, the six-incher, because I want them to see and hear that ball going into the cup and dropping into the bottom. I want that image to accompany them as they work back through the other balls.

As you back up, making putts of increasing length, you strengthen your sense of touch, you feel the contact of putter face and ball, and you construct, piece by piece, a concrete picture of your putt rolling toward the hole. To frame that picture correctly, develop the habit of watching your ball roll from your striking position.

No doubt you'll miss some between the first ball at six inches and the tenth ball at twenty feet. (If you don't, skip on to the next chapter.) That's okay—you can learn from misses as well as makes. The purpose of the drill, remember, is to help you *feel* the relationship between speed and line. So long as you're getting feedback about that relationship, the drill is useful.

The only time you should stop, go back, and start all over is if you make an egregiously bad stab and the ball goes five feet short, past, or way off line. But that won't happen often. I'll bet you'll be surprised at the number of fifteen- and twenty-footers you do make.

This drill won't take all the terror out of your next thirty-foot, right-to-left downhiller on a superfast green—much less guarantee that you'll make it. For that you need to go to the miracles department. But it will help take the sting out of longer putts with a lot of break in them, and—over time—it will reduce the number of three-putt greens (and worse) that currently push your score up.

NO FALSE SIGNALS

A lot of really good putters, when they stop off at the practice green for a couple of minutes before going to the first tee, won't even putt at the hole. They're only rolling the ball a few

Frame-by-Frame. The Ten-Ball Progression Drill helps you develop a mental picture of what happens to a putt on an undulating green.

times for feel and tempo, so they aim at a leaf or make-believe hole. They want to guard against the possibility of a negative thought creeping into their mind after a few misses, such as "Shoot, I can't putt a lick today." But they're also leery about making a bunch because a "Great, I can't miss today" attitude could cause them to get sloppy when they get out on the course. Besides, everybody knows the Golf Gods permit only a certain number of twenty-footers per customer, and nobody wants to waste any of his allotment on the practice green.

DRILL: THE LADDER

Drop four balls onto a flat portion of the practice green. Take your usual stance and stroke one ball about eight to ten feet—not at a hole but to an open area of the green.

Now putt the second ball three feet past the first, the third three feet past the second, and the fourth three feet past the third. Not so easy, is it?

But it will be, the more you work on it.

The Ladder is a drill that helps you feel the swinging force of the club head. To climb the ladder, you don't grip your putter harder or swing it faster—you simply make a slightly longer swing each time.

That principle—"For More Distance, Swing Longer, Not Harder"—is one of the most valuable in golf. It applies not just to your putting but to your full swing as well. When you get right down to it, there are few fundamental differences between a 25-foot putt and a 250-yard drive—the length and shape of the instrument used, the length of the swing, and the involvement of the body in response to the swing.

A variation of this drill, using four or five balls, is to call out the distance of each putt before hitting it—"This one's going just past, this one's going two feet short," and so on. You're looking for solid contact, speed control, and a repeating stroke you can trust.

Once you lock into a repeating stroke, your confidence will build. And once your confidence builds, you'll be surprised at how many key putts start dropping.

DRILL: FRINGE BENEFIT

Imagine a lazy, late afternoon of golf. Nobody's behind you, you're playing by yourself or with a couple of friends, nobody's in a hurry. I know, that may sound like something out of a fairy tale these days, but if you do find yourself in that idyllic situation, take a couple of minutes after holing out and try the Fringe Benefit Drill.

Go to the middle of the green, drop four balls, and putt them in the four directions of the compass just to the fringe, trying to make each ball roll to a stop at the collar.

Everything I teach, from the short putt to the full swing, is based on sensitivity to the weight of the club head as it moves through space. I want you to feel the club head at all times, and I believe that to do so there must be an absence of tension in the swinging elements in particular—your hands, wrists, forearms, shoulder sockets—and the body in general.

The Fringe Benefit Drill helps develop that sensitivity. If you grip your putter too tightly, or if your arms are too tense, you might strike the ball along the line you've chosen, but dollars to doughnuts it will either stop well short of the collar or jump right over it.

The only way you're going to get the ball exactly to the collar is if your body is relaxed, your grip is secure but not tight, and you can feel the club head as it moves first back, then forward into the ball. It will take some practice for the pictures your eyes take of the ball rolling right up to the fringe to be developed, that is, for your sensitivity and your swinging elements to get in harmony.

But if you get good at the Fringe Benefit Drill, I guarantee that it will not only help you manage speed and distance on the greens but also help your part shots and full-swing shots. I think that's a pretty good fringe benefits package, don't you?

A BUCKET OF WATER

You have a thirty-five-footer on a green with more contours than a Miss America Pageant, and if you don't get down in two you're going to lose two bucks and bragging rights for a week. What in the world is this putt going to do?

There are a number of factors involved in reading a green—contour, slope, condition, speed, grain—and, unlike the pros on TV, you don't have all day to figure them out. You can learn a lot as you walk up to the green—often the curvature is more evident from off the green than when you're standing over your putt. You can tell something about the texture of the grass—spongy and slow? crusty and fast?—as you walk up to your ball. And, as with every shot you make, you will determine your final target line by standing *behind* the ball.

I think the best perspective for figuring out what a long putt is going to do is the one that's most often overlooked—from the side.

If you have a long putt and a lot of curvature to deal with, walk half the distance between your ball and the hole, *below the break.* Get back far enough so you can take in the full length of the putt from below it. This enhances your ability to discern the slope and the length of the putt.

Now imagine someone standing at the high point of the break and emptying a bucket of water toward the hole. Which way is that water going to flow? Fix an image of the water spreading out, following the curve of the green, and moving toward the hole. *That's* what's going to happen to your ball.

A GRAIN OF WISDOM

Is the sun shining? Good. There's a quick-and-easy way to determine which way the grain is going, but it depends on sunlight.

Grain growing against you can turn a slightly downhill putt into a flat one. Grain growing away from you can mean a roller-coaster ride right off the green. How to tell which way it's growing?

Walk halfway to the hole along your target line. Look first at the grass between you and the hole, then back toward your ball. Where the shade of green is lighter, the grain is growing away from you. Where it's darker, you're looking into the tiny shadows cast by the grass and the grain is running toward you.

Okay, this isn't going to help much at high noon if you're standing on the equator or on an overcast day. But it's a more reliable tool much of the day than the old rule about grass growing toward the setting sun, which is true for Bermuda grass but not necessarily so for bent.

TWO SCHOOLS

Among average golfers, leaving the ball short of the hole is probably the number one cause of missed putts.

See for yourself. The next time you play, keep a record of the number of missed putts that your foursome leaves short. Also count the number that finish past the hole. Then, the next time you watch a golf tournament on TV, keep comparable stats for the pros. I think you'll be staggered by the difference.

Among the reasons why so many pros today putt like graduates of the Charge It! School of Putting is that "Never up, never in" is as true for putts today as it was when the first Scottish shepherd first said it after leaving one short in a St. Andrews pasture. If you're going to miss, miss long is the Charge It! mantra.

It's true that a ball rolling at a smart pace is going to hold its line better than a ball moving more slowly. Studies have established that the ball will be affected less by imperfections on the green—specifically, in the three-foot-wide circle around the hole, which gets so much wear and tear from golfers standing to retrieve their balls—if the putt is stroked firmly enough to end up, should it not drop, somewhere around twelve to fifteen inches past the hole.

The only problem with the Charge It! philosophy is that some pretty darned good putters don't buy it.

Bobby Jones, Billy Casper, Ben Crenshaw, Jack Nicklaus, and Phil Mickelson have made a few big putts in their careers—and all are alumni of the Die It In the Hole School of Putting. They don't try to "miss short," of course, but they aren't. That is, they try to stroke the ball so that it just gets to the hole . . . and falls in. Jack has told me that he feels the Charge It! philosophy "cuts down the size of the hole" too much for his taste.

Which school of thought you follow will depend a lot on your temperament, your touch, and the amount of time you devote to your putting game. Experiment. See what works best for you.

Nobody wants to leave a putt short, but do you really want to pat yourself on the back for knocking everything two feet past the hole? The idea, remember, is to get the ball *in* the hole.

FEEL

Everybody has sensation. Everybody has touch. Everybody has feel. The trick is learning how to recognize, strengthen, and use those qualities.

Every time I hear somebody say that you can't teach feel, I take him to a green and put a putter in his hands. With a putter in your hands, you're naturally going to think "feel" rather than "power." Bob Toski taught me that feel permeates all parts of the game—or should. That's why I like to teach golf from green to tee.

When you *see* a putt before you actually hit the ball, that visualization has nothing to do with power, only a little to do with mechanics, and everything to do with feel. The best part of it is that the more you do it, the better you get, not only with your putter but with all the other clubs in your bag.

So the next time somebody tells you that you can't teach feel, tell him to meet me at the practice green.

SCORECARD SUMMARY

- The Six Components of Putting: Reading the Green, Aim, Speed Control, Squaring the Putter Face at Impact, Repeating Stroke, Attitude.
- Key Concept: *Let your arms and shoulders be your single producer of speed.*
- Roll ball with your eyes—that is, visualize the speed of the ball as it's rolling toward the hole—*before* placing your putter behind it.
- Don't try to accelerate putter head. Let the pendulum do it for you.
- Watch the ball roll toward the hole from your striking position.
- However much time you currently spend practicing your putting, double it. At *least.*

LESSON 13

HOW *DO* YOU GET TO CARNEGIE HALL?

THE MOST NATURAL-LOOKING GOLFER ever to play the game is Sam Snead. You'd see his swing—so majestic, so flowing and rhythmical—and you'd figure, now *that* has to be a product of nature, not of practice. You'd be wrong.

Oh, he's a gifted natural athlete, blessed with marvelous eye-hand coordination, a great sense of balance, and supple strength. Today, well into his eighties, he still has a golf swing that is a model of pace and timing. But don't think for a minute that Sam Snead came by that beautiful swing by pure, blind, genetic luck. He worked for it.

Many years ago, at a *Golf Digest* panel meeting, Sam told us that if he were to go a week without hitting a golf ball, he'd be afraid he'd have to start all over again. He said that the longest he could remember ever having gone without hitting golf balls was on a hunting trip he took to Africa. After four days, just so he could feel that he was keeping a sense of his swing, he cut a branch off a tree and worked on his swing by hitting elephant dung.

He didn't say how far he hit it, but back then Sam was one of the game's biggest hitters.

The moral of this little tale is that we have to practice to get better at golf. Everybody knows that. Golf and work are both four-letter words. But accepting that in principle is one thing. Doing something about it in practice—that is, by *practicing*—is another. Most of us—and I absolutely include myself here—can't find enough time to *play* as much golf as we'd like. Why should we want to cut into our playing time to *practice*?

We all know the answer, don't we? To make the playing time more fun.

The solution cannot simply be to practice *more,* because your lifestyle may not permit it. The solution is to practice *smart.* To practice less, in some cases, but make it count for more. To practice on changes that will *help* your game, not practice your mistakes. To practice without going to the range or the golf course. Most of all, to practice with the right mental approach.

HOW TO WORK ON YOUR GOLF SWING . . . WITHOUT HITTING A SINGLE BALL

The vast majority of the people I see have limited time to devote to improving their games, no matter how much they love golf. What am I supposed to do, cast them adrift just because they don't wish to devote the time to get their handicap down to single digits? Or give them a few quick fixes, knowing they won't translate into a reliable swing that they can build on? My answer to both questions, just in case you were wondering, is no.

I estimate that, fortunately, about 75 percent of the bad shots in golf are caused by errors of omission and commission *before you swing the golf club.* I say "fortunately" because these are problems you can work on correcting without ever leaving your backyard.

You can work on Grip Pressure, on Feeling the Club Head, on Setup and Posture, on Taking Aim, and on your Pre-Shot Routine without going to the golf course. The golfer who doesn't have time to go to the practice range a couple of times a week can do his golf game a world of good by going out into the backyard and making a dozen Left Leg, Right Toe swings every day. He can practice Setup and Posture in front of the bedroom mirror or work on grip pressure without leaving the office.

A lot of golfers don't like to do practice drills because they feel that it's cutting into time they could spend actually hitting balls. But the truth is, if you're out on the range banging away with your same old swing, you're making a problem that you want to get rid of more permanent. The drills in this chapter can help, even when you don't have much time for practice or play.

Your backyard makes a good learning ground. Or you can work in front of your bedroom mirror. But you do need your hands on the club, both to make your grip second nature and to feel the club head as it moves through space. You also need to practice your Pre-Shot Routine, if only for a few minutes a day.

Most of all, you need to swing your club—and always with a purpose. Have twenty minutes? Go to the backyard, put a couple of tees in the ground about four inches apart, and swing the club head through that gate, just brushing the grass. Once you've made twenty swings without hitting a tee, decrease the distance to three and a half inches. Making those twenty swings through that narrow gate without once hitting a tee will, over time, greatly improve your ability to deliver the club head to the ball.

I spend so much of the year teaching that, like most people, I don't have much time to play the game I love so much. And when I am able to squeeze in a round, it's hard for me to accept that I can't play up to my knowledge level. That doesn't seem right, does it? But it *is* right because the golf club doesn't swing by knowledge. *The golf club swings by feel and awareness ingrained as habit*. For you and for me.

Your hands are the passageway for feel between your body and the club head. Everything has to go through your hands. They are the transmitters that carry an image created in your mind and executed by your body to the club head, which in turn passes the message on to the ball.

So get your hands on your club. Feel the club head's weight. Feel its dynamic swinging force as it's moving through the air. Even if it's in your backyard rather than at a golf course. Even if you're not using balls. All your muscles will stay relaxed and supple when you do this.

Not everyone can go hit balls three times a week. But everyone can do little things every day that increase his feel, sensitivity, and understanding. And that will translate into more fun and lower scores.

SHORT AND SWEET

Time is precious. It's hard to find enough of it for all the things we *need* to do, much less for the things we *want* to do. If golf falls into that latter category for you, use the time you find for it to the best advantage. The average golfer will get a lot more benefit out of three focused, properly spaced, twenty-minute practice sessions that help build good habits than one two-hour-long session in which he merely whacks away mindlessly.

○ ○ ○

LEARNING STATION

Have you ever grown tomatoes? If so, the next time you go to the range to work on your game, stick three of those skinny bamboo sticks you use to stake tomatoes into your golf bag. They're perfect for building a learning station.

Oh, you could use three yardsticks, or three half-inch dowels cut three feet long, or even three golf clubs, although, if you use golf clubs, you'll have to rebuild your learning station every time you decide to hit some balls with one of them.

Lay one of the stakes about two feet in front of your ball along your target line. (If you use a club, make sure the grip end is facing you.) Put another stake about two feet behind your ball, also along the target line. Put the third about two feet alongside the ball, parallel to the other two, so that when you assume your stance the stake nearest your feet will be three or four inches in front of your toes.

All set? Now step back behind your learning station for a reminder about the first rule of aiming, the one we spent so much time on back in Lesson 7, namely, the concept of parallel left.

The first stake—the one in front of your ball—gives you a guideline for where the ball travels after impact. Let your eyes track down that shaft to the target before each swing. The second stake—the one behind your ball—provides a benchmark for the arc the club head follows on the takeaway. The third stake—the one alongside the ball and in front of your toes when you assume your stance—reminds you that, in the basic stance, the correct alignment of your toes is perpendicular to a line running parallel and left of the target line, not directly along the target line.

Right about now you're thinking, This sounds pretty rinky-dink, I've played a lot of golf, I don't need training wheels.

Study Hall. Think of the practice range as a classroom. Wouldn't you want to have your own learning station?

But okay, I'll humor Jim, I'll take those silly stakes with me a couple of times. I'll get used to looking down that forward stake toward my target. Once I get comfortable with that target line–parallel left thing and commit it to habit, though, I'm chucking those stakes so I won't look like some kind of rank amateur who doesn't know how to aim.

Fine, but I'll tell you what to do—go out on a Tuesday or Wednesday before a professional golf tournament and pay a visit to the practice range. Count the number of tour players who set up a learning station of some sort. (True, they'll be using clubs instead of tomato stakes—you wouldn't want to see someone DQ'ed for carrying seventeen clubs because his caddie forgot and stuck the stakes in his bag, would you?)

Perhaps only a few tour players set up a learning station all the time, but *all* of them set one up some of the time. And the reason is simple: tour players know that, no matter how long they've been playing, from time to time they will get out of alignment.

PICK YOUR ROLE MODELS CAREFULLY

Ben Hogan set the all-time standard for practice. Nick Faldo, Tom Kite, and Vijay Singh have come closest among contemporary golfers to matching it. Most professional golfers spend more time at the practice range than playing in tournaments. Makes sense—it's their livelihood, the competition is ferocious, and golf is a demanding game.

There is, of course, one notorious exception to the notion that practice is important: Bruce Lietzke.

If you follow the PGA Tour at all, you know about this wonderful player with the unique attitude toward the game. Lietzke, who has won thirteen tournaments and nearly

$6 million since joining the tour in 1975, competes in only fifteen or sixteen events a year. He'd rather spend time with his family than spend months on the road. He doesn't usually play in the U.S. Open or the British Open because they interfere with his kids' Little League schedules. He always plays in the Players Championship so he can fish the ponds and lakes at Sawgrass, and he never, ever—or, at least, hardly ever—practices.

There's a famous story about Lietzke and his reputation for not touching a club for weeks unless he is playing in a tournament. Seems that his caddie decided to test this reputation. So, just before one of Lietzke's hiatuses from the tour, the caddie stuck a banana inside the top cover of his golf bag before packing it up. No way, figured the caddie, that his boss was going to go six weeks without playing, and this would prove it. Wrong. Have you ever seen what a banana looks—and smells—like after six weeks inside a golf bag? Ask Bruce Lietzke's caddie.

Fact is, Bruce played golf almost daily from age ten until his mid-twenties, and he obviously created some pretty doggone good habits that have served him well. Needless to say, even though it's obviously worked for him, I can't recommend the Bruce Lietzke approach to the concept of practice, although I do think his approach to the concept of family is outstanding.

WARM-UP VERSUS PRACTICE

There's a big difference between a warm-up session and a training or practice session.

With the warm-up session, you're going right to the golf course. You're working on your rhythm. You're working on the feel of your swing. You're not tearing your swing apart.

You shouldn't be thinking of any of the parts. You're trying to connect with the whole swing, your setup, and your routine.

A training or practice session is one in which I am really going to work on the *segments* of my swing. I'm going to work on positions. I'm going to be thinking a lot about mechanics and technique. I'm going to be finding ways to improve and create good habits.

Too many people go to the golf course and, fifteen minutes before their tee time, start tearing their swing apart, trying to incorporate some tip they read in a golf book the night before. That's just fine if they only plan to practice, that is, to *work* on golf instead of *play* it.

Take a tip from the tour players, who like to warm up, play, *then* practice—and build the practice session around what they learned on the course that day.

Practice is about mechanics. Playing is about feel, rhythm—and the target.

MORE THAN A MIND JOB

No one believes more strongly than I that the mind is the place to start building a golf game. Without the right concepts and mind-set, a person will flounder around, mixing good shots and bad, without any understanding of what caused which. A repeating swing is as likely as back-to-back aces.

A concert pianist came through a Nicklaus-Flick Golf School once. I asked her, "How many hours a day do you practice?"

She answered, "About four or five hours a day even when I'm playing a concert tour." To learn the music? Hardly. To internalize it, to make it her own? Now you're on the right track.

If I miss one day, she added, no big deal. Two days, and she could tell the difference in her playing. Three days, her husband could tell. Four days or more? "I don't know for sure because I've never tested it," she said. "But I fear the audience could tell."

The great dancer Mikhail Baryshnikov, who loves golf, was a student in one of our schools. I asked him, at the height of his career, how much time he spent practicing when he wasn't performing.

"Well, I would typically spend four to five hours a day while learning a new move," he told me. "And I would practice some every day."

To perform at the level he demanded of himself, he had to maintain his training habits. He knew the moves—in some cases, he choreographed them—but it was not enough to have the moves in his mind. He had to train his body. There was just no room for compromise.

A lot of people—maybe most of us—want our mind to train our body without going through the physical effort, the part that takes so much time. That's understandable. But thinking the right thoughts doesn't guarantee physical performance. That's the first step, not the whole journey. If you haven't hit enough golf balls, and you haven't developed a habit that will repeat itself, how can you expect to hit good shots consistently on the golf course? By that line of reasoning, if you can read music, you should be able to play all the musical instruments and all the melodies ever written.

The Golf Gods are not going to let that happen. If you're going to get good in golf, there must be a compatible, working arrangement between your mind-set and your physical execution.

To correlate them takes time. Is there a shortcut? If I learn one, you'll be the first to know.

TARGET PRACTICE

Practice ranges can lull you into false confidence. No out-of-bounds left, no trees right, no water anywhere—and if you hit a bad shot, you just pull another ball from the pile and take another whack.

Always have a target while practicing. Keep score—for instance, how many out of ten shots hit in the target zone? Make the practice range as much like the course as possible.

Ever see a basketball player working on his jump shot without a basket? Absolutely not. Well, a golfer needs a target just as much. Having a target makes you competitive, encourages you to work on your alignment and setup, and keeps you focused. Without a target, you're just getting a little light exercise.

PLAYING GROUND VERSUS TRAINING GROUND

Standing next to the tee, waiting your turn to hit, in the middle of a fiercely contested two-dollar match, you begin to think about what's wrong with your golf swing. Your mind overflows with swing thoughts. You flash back to all the golf tips you've read in all the golf magazines the last twelve months. You're wondering if that big loop that Trevino does will help cure you from coming over the top. You think about driving your right knee forward on the downswing. You know you need to work on letting your hands drop so the club can get into the slot. Swivel your head back on address like Nicklaus?

Waggle like Floyd? Take an outrageous practice swing like Pavin? Whistle like Zoeller? Dress like Stewart?

Stop.

All those thoughts—at least some of them—are perfectly appropriate for the Training Ground, where analysis is vital to change. But for the Playing Ground, analysis leads to paralysis—or worse.

When you're training, you are trying to alert your mind, your sensitivity for what can go wrong. When you're playing, you should focus on what is *right* about your golf swing for positive reinforcement of your only goal: getting the ball in the hole in the fewest number of strokes.

The Training Ground should be dominated by the conscious mind, the Playing Ground by the subconscious.

On the Training Ground, you're fragmenting your golf swing and working on individual positions and segments. On the Playing Ground, you're emphasizing the flow of the whole swing.

On the Training Ground, you employ a conscious thought process that from time to time interferes with your rhythm. On the Playing Ground, you're trying to feel the club head and get a sense of rhythm to enable you to use the instrument to get the ball into the target area.

On the Training Ground—the practice range—you tell yourself what to do. On the Playing Ground—the golf course—you play with pictures and feel, not verbal instructions.

When you practice, you want to be guided by your conscious mind to implement changes that you can develop into habits. When you play, you do not want your conscious mind to interfere with the habits you have developed.

❍ ❍ ❍

BASIC TRAINING

The high handicapper—someone who rarely breaks one hundred without a couple of mulligans—can knock five to ten strokes off his game in a month just by working conscientiously on three things: posture, grip pressure, and alignment. If you stand straight but not rigid, then bend first at the hips, and then slightly flex the knees, allowing your weight to balance on the balls of your feet; if you hold the club with the appropriate grip pressure (Fingers Secure, Arms Relaxed); and if you set up parallel left of the target, you're going to hit fewer disaster shots. And the disaster shots—the ones that end up wet or OB or playing wood tag—are the main difference between a guy who can't break one hundred and the bogey golfer.

To you low handicappers who think that working on posture, grip pressure, and alignment is a little too elementary for you, think again. When Jack Nicklaus came to see me just before the 1996 Tradition, he'd been having trouble getting his tee shots to go where he wanted them, so we spent our first hour together working on just one thing: alignment. (P.S.: Jack won the tournament.)

You can never practice enough making sure you have the correct posture. You can never practice enough making sure you have the correct grip pressure. And you can never practice enough on your alignment. Just remember: these three things really will knock strokes off your score almost immediately.

If you find a drill that's really difficult for you, it probably means that's the drill you need the most.

FEEDBACK

On every shot Tom Watson hits at the practice range, he watches the ball's flight, its bounce, and its roll. It gives him information about his golf swing, about how he delivered the club head to the ball. The average guy hits a ball on the range and is staring down at his next one before the first hits the ground. Most tour players pay close attention to their ball flight to confirm that they are getting a consistent trajectory. The lesson? There's something to learn from every aspect of your game. Help build your feel and understanding of your swing by learning from your ball flight. The ball will not lie to you.

WHO'S PLAYING TODAY?

Every time you play, you have to find out what kind of game you have that day. Your concept hasn't changed, but today's body isn't identical to last weekend's body. Some days, for instance, your fingers are puffy, and that will affect your grip pressure. Some days, you're anxious rather than calm or rushed rather than relaxed.

Two constants for the day should be established immediately: your aim and your grip pressure. If you do that, you have the building blocks on which to base your swing—with whichever body and mind show up that day.

TEE IT UP

When you're working on something specific at the practice range—especially when you're working on a swing change—tee the ball up slightly. You're not trying to score, you're trying to get information about your swing. Teeing the ball up removes one impediment—the earth—from the equation and lets you focus on the mechanics and the feel of your swing.

CLUB SELECTION

Most people go to the range, pull out their driver, and start whaling away until the bucket's empty. I recommend starting with a five iron or a six iron. You're more likely to make a controlled swing with a middle iron, plus you will get some feedback regarding your ball flight. If you take a more lofted club, you hit so low on the ball that all you get is backspin instead of side spin; there's no curvature to tell you how you delivered the club head to the ball. You don't learn as much about your swing for the day.

50/50

If your average score is ninety, then approximately 60 to 70 percent of your shots on the golf course are made from inside one hundred yards. The percentage is a little lower for better golfers, a little higher for golfers on the other side of one hundred.

So how do you allocate your time on the practice range among the clubs in your bag?

Do a quick survey the next time you're at the range. On second thought, don't bother: I've done it for you. About 75 percent of the golfers are hitting their driver. And for many of them, the driver is the *only* club they hit.

It's pretty obvious what's wrong with this picture. The tour player spends 50 percent of his practice time—or more—working on his short game. The average golfer spends 75 percent of his time ignoring it.

You don't need to practice tap-ins, but my guess is the rest of your short game needs more attention than you're giving it. I recommend that you allocate 50 percent of your practice time to short-game shots and 50 percent to full-swing shots. (I'd say make it 60–40, but I know you won't do it.)

The payoff will come on your scorecard.

FLICK'S TOP 10 DRILLS

Yeah, I know—drills are boring, you just want to hit some balls. So what if I convince you that a few well-constructed, focused drills can help you hit balls *better*? Here are ten drills that fall into that category:

1. Left Foot, Right Toe

Take your usual setup, then pull back your right foot and touch your toe against the ground just enough to maintain balance. With your full weight on your left leg, make your swing and hit the ball. The more you tend to pull the ball, the more you bring your right toe back behind your left heel.

This is a terrific drill if your body or legs have been outracing your club head. If you lurch forward with your body, you won't get to the ball and you'll very likely fall on your butt. Left Foot, Right Toe keeps your body at home until your arms and hands swing the club head through the ball, turning your body in the process. This drill is also great for instilling an inside-along-the-target-line to inside swing path.

Learn to make solid contact with the Left Foot, Right Toe swing and you may never slice the ball again.

2. Up-and-Down

Take ten balls to the practice green. Chip or pitch onto the green and putt out—every time. Set a target score based on your skill level—thirty? twenty-five? Don't quit until you make that number. Eventually your target will be par—twenty.

Having a goal makes *practicing* more fun. Finishing each hole ingrains a *playing* attitude.

3. Love Power

Take a big, full swing with your driver—and try to hit your ball just 100 yards. Then try to hit one 150, 200, and finally as far as you can. This is the drill that Davis Love, Jr., used to teach Davis III the importance of rhythm in the golf swing. It's a lot tougher than it sounds because you're so accustomed to one speed with your driver. What the drill does is demonstrate how the hands and arms and the body—the swinging elements and the turning elements, remember?—must work in harmony to create the club-head speed needed for the requisite distance.

4. Four-Step

Grab a mid-iron, tee up your ball, and take your regular stance. Then:

1. Cock your wrists and lay your club on your right shoulder *without* changing your spine angle. Fingers secure, arms relaxed and close to your sides.
2. Turn your torso, with your weight moving over your right leg. The turn should be about 90 degrees, with left shoulder moving behind ball.
3. Lift the club into the desired position of your normal backswing, that is, shaft parallel to the ground and to the target line. Your hands should be under the shaft with the club face square and about top-of-your-head high.
4. Here comes the hard part. With hands and wrists still cocked, drop your arms down toward your right pants leg while holding your torso and shoulders turned. Think of this as a rehearsal of the first half of your forward swing.

> Do it three times, letting your hands stop just above the right knee each time. Then, take one final swing—this time, a complete one—with no change in effort level, and let your hands return to your starting position at address so that your club head can strike your ball squarely from the inside. Don't worry about your follow-through—the swing's momentum will take care of it.

Of all the drills I use regularly, Four-Step is probably the hardest, but it also does the most for you. It helps you find the correct position for the shaft and the club head at the top of the backswing. It also introduces a feeling for the proper order of movement in the change of direction. And it helps you understand and feel the correct path of the club in the first half of the forward swing.

That last point is especially important because it's precisely in that first half of the forward swing that so many golfers meet their Waterloo. They let their hands run out away from their bodies, creating an outside-in swing path that becomes a one-way street to a slice (if the club face stays open) or a pull-hook (if they manage to close it).

The Four-Step is the best medicine I know to cure that common malady and to teach the proper routing of the golf club in the forward swing.

How important is routing the club on that inside path? Well, Byron Nelson told me once that he never carried anything in his right front pocket when he played because he didn't want anything, *anything,* to get in the way of his hands as they brought his club head toward the ball.

As I said, the Four-Step is hard. Don't expect to make solid ball contact, at least not at first. That will come as you meld the four steps together into a coherent whole.

5. Right Hand Off After Impact

Take your regular swing, but release your right hand after impact, allowing your left arm to fold naturally so that the club's shaft ends up on your left shoulder.

This drill helps train your right arm and right shoulder not to overpower your swing.

If you try Right Hand Off After Impact and experience difficulty in getting your right hand to come off, it means you're overpowering or overcontrolling the club with your right hand and arm. Once you learn to do this drill effortlessly, you will have reached the proper balance between left side–right side control.

6. Chair

Place a sturdy folding chair beside your ball where you would normally take your stance. Sit on the right front edge of the chair facing your ball. Bend your right leg behind you to get it out of the way. With the ball on a tee, take a normal swing—not that I'm suggesting you usually swing from a seated position—with a driver. Use half swings at first, until you can comfortably find your ball.

The goal here is to give you a feel for the swinging action of the golf club, to promote freedom in the arms, and to teach hand action.

7. Eyes Closed

Regular stance, mid-iron, ball on tee—only just before you swing, close your eyes.

Sounds crazy, I know, but this drill is wonderful for helping develop feel for your club head throughout the swing and for making you aware of changes in grip pressure. Your sense of touch has to carry a bigger load. You also discover pretty fast that you need a gentle, rhythmic swing to find your ball.

The Four-Step Drill. Not sure where the shaft and the club head should be at the top of the backswing? Want to rehearse the order of movement at the change of direction? Like to implant the feel of bringing the club down in the proper arc? Well, then, the Four-Step is just the drill for you.

My prediction is that you'll be surprised at how often you do manage to hit it. That's why I'll give this drill to a guy who has a better swing than he thinks he has.

8. Right Hand Alone/Left Hand Alone

For this drill you need to have the ball on a tee and a mid-iron in your hands. Or hand.

First grip the club with both hands to make sure they're positioned properly, then remove your left hand altogether and make a nice, rhythmic swing using only your right hand. Take the club to your customary, desired position at the top of the backswing. While doing so, feel your right shoulder moving around and behind the ball. (Remember, no "tray position" at the top. Your right wrist should be under your shaft, not bent out as if holding a tray.)

Now do the same thing, only this time remove your right hand and make your swing with only your left hand. At the top of your backswing, be aware of your wrist staying under your shaft and cocking naturally. Also be aware of the club approaching the ball from the inside on the forward swing.

This is a good drill for teaching the different but complementary roles played by your two hands during the golf swing. Jack Nicklaus uses Right Hand Alone when he feels as if he needs to work on getting the club deeper around him. The average golfer might benefit more from Left Hand Alone because it helps him recognize the inside path he needs to draw his ball. Just be sure to let the left elbow fold naturally after impact so that the club head can release and the shaft ends up on your left shoulder.

9. Back to Target

From your regular stance, leave your arms and club in their normal address position as you pivot on your left foot and turn

Drawing Board. Back to Target is a terrific drill for the golfer who's trying to learn to draw the ball.

your torso and feet to the right so that your back is to the target. Now take a swing, using your arms and hands in normal routing to make the ball go to the target. Take easy half swings at first until you become adept at finding the ball.

The purpose of Back to Target is to impart a feeling for the arms controlling the change of direction in the golf swing without the body rushing forward first. Back to Target also requires your arms and club head to pass through the impact area in an arc that encourages a draw.

I often prescribe this drill for a golfer whose left arm is too tense because you can't complete the swing from this position without correctly folding your left arm after impact.

10. Balance Beam

The Balance Beam is actually a post-swing drill. That's right: *post*-swing. Right about now you're thinking, What does this guy mean, "post-swing" drill? That I should practice wrapping my club around a tree?

No, most golfers are born with a pretty good idea of how to do that. And I'm not suggesting a way to practice celebrating a good shot. We all know how to do that, too. What I'm talking about is a way to ingrain a good habit, to groove a good idea.

Impact has been made, the ball is aloft, and you've just completed your follow-through—hold it! Right there, hold your balance at the very end of your follow-through until the ball stops rolling. The other members of your foursome will instantly accuse you of posing, so do this drill only when you're on the practice range—at the far end, by yourself.

But this is no gag—there is a purpose to the Balance Beam.

For starters, if you *can* hold your balance it means your body is *in* balance and has been through the swing. That's an important feeling because if your body is not in balance through the swing, any good shot you hit will be a lucky one. If you're in balance, chances are your hands, arms, and club head worked in harmony through impact and into your finish.

AND ONE MORE

Now, one more thing: when you've completed your shot, twirl your club. Ever notice how many pro golfers do that? They hit a good shot, they watch it, then give the club a little twirl before handing it back to their caddie. They may be only partly aware of what they're doing, but think a minute—what do you *have* to have to twirl a golf club?

Relaxed hands.

What better way to finish a good golf shot than the way you started it, with relaxed hands?

So go ahead—make my day.

Twirl your club.

SCORECARD SUMMARY

- Key Concept: *Because about 75 percent of bad shots in golf are caused by errors of omission (and commission) made prior to swinging the golf club, you can work on your game without going to the practice range.*
- Three properly focused twenty-minute sessions per week are more helpful in forming good habits than one two-hour session.
- Build your own learning station at the practice range.
- Practice is about mechanics. Playing is about feel and rhythm.
- Three biggies you can work on without hitting a ball: posture, grip pressure, alignment.

LESSON 14

THE BODY SHOP

TWENTY YEARS AGO, WHEN you went to a baseball game, what did you see the players doing fifteen minutes before the national anthem? Nothing, mostly. They'd be back in the clubhouse, or sitting in the dugout, or maybe having a game of slow catch. Nothing at all strenuous, nothing too serious. Now what do you see? Guys on the outfield grass doing elaborate stretching drills. The same is true in football, basketball, and other sports, where lackadaisical calisthenics have given way to serious pregame stretching.

Something similar has happened in golf. Used to be, the only stretching tour pros did was reaching for the pretzels at the hotel bar well into the night before an early-morning tee time. Gary Player was the exception that proved the rule: he was the first to take physical conditioning seriously. Nowadays, the Cintenela Fitness Trailer is a fixture at PGA Tour and PGA Senior Tour events, and players are in much better physical condition than they used to be, especially when it comes to flexibility.

Mike Malaska, a senior instructor at the Nicklaus-Flick Golf School, developed a set of flexibility exercises to kick off each day's classes. They serve two purposes, the first and most obvious of which is to get people loose and to emphasize the need for flexibility in swinging a golf club. Stretching every day helps you get the most out of your golf game. And it helps you get the most out of the rest of your life.

But having students at the golf school do the flexibility drills also gives me an opportunity to see any swing problems that might be related to body conditioning factors. For example, if I'm trying to get more turn out of a guy, and he doesn't have the flexibility to turn without lifting up, then trying to get him turned more will produce a *less* effective golf swing. Similarly, once students come to realize what effect conditioning and flexibility limitations are going to have on their golf swing, they often become motivated to take corrective action.

Take Tom Lehman. Had himself a pretty good year in 1996, didn't he? Well, he'll tell you that one significant reason for that terrific year was the work he put in over the winter of 1995–1996 to increase the flexibility in his hips. Mike Malaska developed a personal exercise program for Tom, who worked hard at it, really hard. Boy, did it pay off. The increased flexibility helped him to be able to swing back to the inside after impact and to finish around his body, hallmarks of the Professional Swing. This diminished his need for club-head rotation and helped give him a more consistent, repeatable swing. This past winter, Mike adjusted Tom's program to include rope skipping, not only to provide aerobic conditioning but to help increase Tom's agility.

Flexibility is necessary so that our bodies can respond to the swinging of our arms. Without that flexibility, we have to make an effort to make our bodies respond to that swinging motion, and that effort creates extra possibilities for something to go wrong. The extra effort interrupts the easy rhythm that we're trying to achieve, it changes the sequence of movements, and it often creates tension, which interferes with the overall swinging process and feel for the club head.

THE BIG EIGHT

The following flexibility and strength exercises take a total of about fifteen to twenty minutes a day to perform. When doing them, remember some basic stretching rules: warm up your muscles a few minutes (walking rapidly in place, for instance) before stretching; hold stretches fifteen to twenty seconds; never bounce or strain; always do two repetitions because on your second stretch you're usually able to stretch even further.

1. Club Press

Stand with feet shoulder-width apart, back straight, chin up. Grip shaft of golf club with both hands, one at each end, with backs of hands facing up, and hold club at eye level close to your face. Press hands slightly toward center and extend arms directly away from you, then bring back. Do twenty times.

Think of this as a golfer's bench press, only not on a bench and with only a pound or so of weight. But as you extend your arms, bring your elbows back as far as you can, all the while maintaining hand tension toward the center. I guarantee you'll feel some heat in the middle of your back, where your shoulder muscles are moored.

2. Shoulder Rolls

Stand with arms hanging freely at your sides, back straight, chin up. Lift shoulders and roll them forward and around. Use slow, fluid motion. Do twenty. Reverse direction, do twenty more.

The simplest of all flexibility exercises, this one also gives the most instant gratification. Feels great, doesn't it? Do it anywhere: in your office, in an elevator, before each tee shot. Terrific while sitting in an airplane, too.

3. Wings of Man

Hold arms out to side, parallel to ground, with thumbs pointed forward and palms down. Move arms in tight circles toward your thumbs. Do twenty, making circles a little larger each time. Feel your shoulders heat up? Next, turn thumbs toward rear, palms up, and reverse direction of circles. Do twenty.

This exercise loosens and strengthens your shoulders and your rotator cuffs.

4. Cheek Press

Press knuckles of both hands against temples with thumbs at base of cheeks. Keeping knuckles on face, touch elbows in front, then extend them back as far as you can. Do twenty.

This is another exercise that increases the mobility and the flexibility in your shoulders and upper arms.

5. Cat and Dog

On hands and knees, chin up, eyes forward. Arch spine and roll chin toward chest; hold for a few seconds (the Cat). Lower spine toward ground and raise chin; hold for a few seconds (the Dog). Exhale when doing the Cat; inhale when doing the Dog. Repeat.

This increases flexibility in lower back and hips. (If you're fairly limber, try this when you're finished: straighten legs and bend at hips, trying to get heels to touch ground. Call it the Advanced Cat.)

6. Runner's Stretch

Feet side by side, step forward on left foot about eighteen inches. Keep heels flat on ground, legs straight, trunk erect, chin up, back straight. Hold on to the back of a chair or a golf cart for stability. Now slowly bend forward at hips, letting arms hang down to ground, back still straight and chin up, until you begin to feel stretch in left hamstring and upper calf. Hold for twenty seconds. Slowly return to upright position. Repeat. Then do two repeats with right foot forward.

Be sure to keep back straight and chin up throughout this exercise; heels on ground; no bend in knees.

This stretches your hamstrings and calves. Tight hamstrings are a prime cause of lower back trouble, so the Runner's Stretch can be the golfer's best friend, at least in the exercise department.

7. Trunk Twist

Stand with feet shoulder-width apart, back straight, chin up, and arms held straight out from sides. Slowly turn from waist as far as you can to right while keeping eyes forward. Hold for twenty seconds, then return to starting position. Repeat exercise, this time turning left. Do at least two trunk twists to each side.

Notice how much farther you're able to turn the second time—instant proof that flexibility exercises work. Also note the difference, if any, in how much you can turn to one side as opposed to the other. Many right-handed people find they can turn farther, and easier, to their right than to their left; vice versa for lefties. What does this information tell you about your forward swing? It tells me that lack of flexibility is one reason so many golfers tend to lift up out of their swings—it's the only way they can complete them because of limited flexibility.

8. Sitting Trunk Flex

Sit on floor with legs extended in front of you, back erect, chin up, hands on floor next to your hips to brace you. Bring right foot up and place it on outside of left knee. Swing left arm over and rest it against right leg. Move right hand back on floor behind you so that straightened right arm is brace. Slowly twist upper body to right and turn head to look over right shoulder, making sure to keep back straight throughout. Turn as far as you can and hold for twenty seconds. Return to starting position, then reverse position, this time looking over left shoulder.

Don't worry—it only looks complicated. And I promise you won't end up as a permanent human pretzel. This exercise will increase your ability to get more turn in your backswing and to maintain your spine angle on your forward swing. For right-handers, the twist to the right will improve flexibility for your backswing, while the left twist helps your forward swing. Vice versa for left-handers, as usual. Your goal during this stretch—and it will take you some time to achieve unless you are in really good shape—is to have your shoulders lined up with the leg that's flat on the floor.

BOTTOMS UP

When playing in a tournament, Jack Nicklaus and Gary Player, two of the smartest golfers ever to play the game, will drink a cup of water on almost every tee, no matter where they are, no matter what the conditions. It's not a matter of thirst—it's a matter of preparation. In certain climates, you can become dehydrated before you even get thirsty. Dehydration causes loss of focus, tightening of muscles, and fatigue, any of which can destroy your rhythm. Hot weather or cold, when in doubt, drink.

GIVE ME STRENGTH

The oldest joke in golf—and that's saying a lot—has a gorilla hitting a 275-yard drive straight down the middle on a long par five, then hitting a 275-yard fairway wood to the fringe, then pulling out his putter, lining up his eagle putt, and stroking the ball—another 275 yards. (Okay, I *thought* maybe you might have heard it.)

Now, in addition to being the obvious source of golf's oldest cliché—Drive for Show/Putt for Dough—and suggesting that gorillas don't have much touch around the green, this little parable offers a cautionary note about strength training.

Trying to build strength is risky business for a golfer. A couple of off-seasons ago, Nick Faldo spent the winter bulking up by lifting weights—he thought the added muscle would give him more length—and went on to have his worst year in over a decade. So he cut back on the weights, trimmed back on the bulk, and returned to being one of the two or three best golfers in the world. (P.S. He never did get the extra ten yards he was looking for, probably because he sacrificed flexibility for muscle mass.)

Golf is not a game of power, remember? Otherwise, how do you explain Corey Pavin?

But take a look at Tom Kite's forearms, the only part of the man's entire body that would suggest he might be an athlete. Popeye would be envious. Also, I have never met a good golfer who didn't have really strong fingers and hands.

I believe a judicious strength program that focuses on the hands, wrists, and forearms makes sense for most golfers, men or women. Here are six exercises that will strengthen your primary golf muscles. You can do them as often as you want.

1. Finger Rolls

Hold hands in front of you, palms facing, thumbs up. Curl fingers—not thumbs—back toward palms. Make certain not to bend fingers at knuckle that joins to hand; bend at forward two knuckles only.

You can do finger rolls whenever you want, wherever you want—at your desk, sitting at a stoplight, waiting for the bottleneck at a par three to clear. The stronger your fingers, the lighter your grip can be on your club.

2. Towel Twist

Arms extended in front of you, grip doubled hand towel so that hands are about four inches apart, backs of hands facing up. Twist in opposite directions, back and forth, as hard as you can. Do as many sets of ten as you wish, wherever you wish.

This strengthens your wrists and forearms. You can buy a clublike device specially designed for this exercise from many golf equipment catalogues. The towel works just as well.

3. Windshield Wiper

Elbows against sides, hold club in each hand in front of you, perpendicular to ground. Raise and lower clubs from side to side, bringing them parallel to ground each time. Do ten for each side.

This strengthens the forearms and the wrists without building up the biceps and triceps.

4. Club Twirl

Arms hanging down against sides, hold club in each hand, parallel to ground. Roll wrists and twirl the clubs in circles. Do ten in one direction, then ten in the other.

This exercise increases strength and flexibility in the wrists. You'll probably find that one wrist doesn't hinge as well as the other. For right-handers, the weaker wrist will be the left wrist and vice versa.

5. Basic Crunch

Flat on back on floor, legs bent at knees at 90-degree angle, hands folded on chest. Lift shoulders up until they completely clear floor. Keep neck and back straight; don't roll chin toward chest. Do as many as you comfortably can to begin, and build from there. Hold last one for twenty seconds.

This is not about developing washboard abs, though that would be a nice plus if you really work at it. This is about strengthening your abdominal muscles and thereby reducing your susceptibility to lower back strain. Golf can be tough on your back. Strong abdominal muscles are the back's best support system.

There are almost as many variations and advanced versions of the basic crunch as there are putters. Just remember one thing: to guard against injuring your back, you should never, ever do crunches or sit-ups with your legs stretched out flat against the floor.

6. Walk

Everywhere, anywhere you possibly can. Briskly. Around the block. Before or after lunch. At the gym on a treadmill in bad weather. Instead of elevators and escalators when practical. And always, *ALWAYS*, on the golf course.

Your legs ever get tired, maybe a little wobbly, at the end of a round, particularly on a hot day? Bet your swing got wobbly, too. Remember—the golf swing needs support from the ground up.

INCENTIVE PROGRAM

I'm not going to try to con you into believing that doing half an hour of flexibility and strength exercises every day is a whole gang of fun, although, once they become routine, I don't think you'll find them a burden. The trick is getting started, and here I think I can offer you a pretty good incentive:

How about two strokes a round off your score without even having to swing a club?

Think about it. Have you ever thrown away a couple of strokes on the first three or four holes because you weren't quite loosened up? My guess is the answer is yes. It certainly is for most golfers. Maybe you hit a few balls at the practice range. Maybe you make a few rehearsal swings on the tee. But that doesn't help because your body isn't flexible enough to begin with. A regular stretching program could save you those strokes you're wasting now because you're too tight.

What happens when people ask their bodies to do things they are not in condition to do easily is that extra effort must be expended, thereby creating tension. For instance, your spine angle as you swing back and forward through the ball should not change from the original address position: back straight, chin up, body bent forward from hips so that arms hang down from shoulder sockets, knees slightly flexed.

But if your body is not sufficiently flexible, this is probably what will happen: you will come up out of your spine angle during the backswing and the forward swing, rotating the shoulders in advance of the club head, which is then rerouted over the top on an outside-to-inside plane. The result? A pull-hook or a severe slice, depending on the position of the club face at impact.

So, before going to the Training Ground or the Playing Ground, don't you think you should spend a little time in the body shop?

SCORECARD SUMMARY

- Key Concept: *Flexibility is essential if your body is to respond to the swinging of your arms.*
- Fifteen to twenty minutes a day of flexibility exercises will do a lot more for your game than that new titanium driver you've had your eyes on.
- Remember, the body sustains and develops itself through motion.

LESSON 15

THE GAME OF GOLF IS 90 PERCENT MENTAL. THE OTHER 10 PERCENT IS . . . MENTAL.

THE GAME OF GOLF begins in your mind. More than athletic ability, more than technique, more than practice or equipment or anything else, the mind-set—or attitude—that you bring to the game determines not only the enjoyment you will derive from it but also the level of proficiency you will achieve.

If you come to me for help with your golf game, the first thing I'm going to try to find out is what kind of attitude you bring to the first tee. I try to crawl inside your head. I try to discover what you're feeling and what you're thinking. And whether they are in sync.

In over four decades of teaching, I have discovered that the point of origin—point zero—of the golf game is attitude. Before I can begin to prescribe changes in your grip or swing or anything, I need to understand something about the way you respond to the idea of change itself.

Are you accurate in your assessment of your skills? Are your expectations realistic given your lifestyle? Are you willing to experiment? Are you willing to accept temporary discomfort in order to form new habits? And, perhaps most important, how do you react to failure and disappointment?

Every athlete who competes wants to win. It's natural. It's also natural that coming up just short is going to hurt. Has to. Would you agree that coming in second over and over when your goal is to come in first could be potentially devastating?

Well, consider this—the golfer who holds the all-time record for the number of second-place finishes on the PGA Tour is none other than Mr. Jack William Nicklaus. Finishing just short of his goal fifty-nine times (plus another four seconds on the Senior Tour) didn't devastate him for the simple reason that he drew strength and understanding from disappointment rather than self-pity or despair.

And when Tom Lehman lost the 1996 U.S. Open on the seventy-second hole by a single stroke, he didn't curl up and whimper, did he? What he did was go out the next month and win the British Open.

The moral here is pretty obvious: to gain success, you must be able to learn from failure.

Some people give up on themselves when things are going tough. Others celebrate too quickly when things are going well. I believe it's critical to develop habits that see you through either side of the spectrum, whether it be good news or bad news in life, good performance or bad performance on the golf course.

The honest truth is that attitude, even more than athletic talent or a picture-perfect swing, determines the level of success you achieve. That's true in golf, and it's also true in life.

Please understand that failure is not fatal—in golf, it's an essential part of the learning and improvement process. If you experience failure and learn from it, then you can continue to grow. If you experience failure and feel sorry for yourself and wallow in your own self-pity, you're not going to be successful in life and you're not going to be successful in golf. Crybabies and whiners never reach their full potential, but not for the reasons they think.

A missed shot is not a failure. A missed shot is an opportunity to learn. Think of failure as an opportunity to learn. That's what golf is all about, and that's what life is all about. You have to be able to step back and assess—honestly and accurately—what you need to do to get better. First you precisely define the problem. Next you identify the solution. Then you work to implement it.

A few years ago I was talking to the men's and women's golf teams at Texas Christian University, and I said, "You'll never be a good player until you learn how to lose." Now, I wasn't referring to being a "good loser," although I certainly believe that a person should accept losing with grace and respect for his opponent. I was talking about being a "smart loser," about learning from the loss and building on what you learn.

To be the best player your talent permits, you've got to be your own coach. My goal as a teacher is to give you the tools to diagnose your game, prescribe treatment as needed, and monitor your progress. In other words, to be self-reliant.

Now, I know that in today's world, where so many people are looking to blame their problems on somebody or something else, the term "self-reliance" must sound terribly old-fashioned. I guess it is. But I also know that self-reliance is one of the bedrock elements of golf. You have no pinch hitters, no substitutes, and no one else to blame in golf other than yourself. It's just you and the game.

Yes, I know that golf got its name because all the other four-letter words were taken. No sport is more frustrating. But none, in my view, is more personally rewarding, provided that you come to it with the proper attitude.

IF YOU WANT TO BE COMFORTABLE, DON'T BOTHER GETTING OFF THE COUCH

A lot of times people will come to me and say they want to improve their game, and we'll start working on some things, and then they'll tell me, "That doesn't feel right. That feels strange. That feels uncomfortable."

They're absolutely right. If they've been playing golf with a posture that doesn't let their arms and club swing freely, an alignment that bears little or no relationship to their target, and a grip that prevents them from bringing the club head squarely against the ball, then the things I ask them to do will not feel right. They will feel strange. And they will *certainly* feel uncomfortable.

A person derives comfort from the habit he already has. And if that's the one habit you've got to get rid of to improve your golf swing, then you've got to feel awkward for a while. What makes change so tough in golf is that our most ingrained bad habits are the last to go and the first to come back.

Now, that doesn't mean you go out on the golf course and change your grip or your setup or your whatever at every tee. You don't work on any major change while you're on the golf course. You do it at the Training Ground. Changing an old habit requires a conscious thought process, and you're not out on the golf course to think about the different pieces and parts of your golf game. You're out there to make a score.

If you commit yourself to a major swing change to help your game, you are committing yourself to making something unfamiliar become familiar, that is, to creating a *new* habit. That requires an investment of patience, determination, and time. And it requires acceptance of the fact that, until that new habit takes hold, you're not going to feel as comfortable as you would like.

I look people right in the eye and say, "I don't give a damn whether you're comfortable or not, but I really, *really* care if you are correct."

Comfort is based on where you are coming from. To get better in golf, you need to be more interested in where you are going—and willing to accept being uncomfortable for a while in order to get there.

SWING THOUGHTS

Students frequently ask me to give them a swing key, something to take on the golf course and think about when they set up to execute a shot. I tell them, "Hell, the last thing I want you doing when you're standing over your ball is thinking and giving yourself verbal commands."

For one thing, I'm leery of a single, conscious thought that might introduce tension at precisely the moment when your body should be guided by routine and habit. On the Training Ground, when you're working on some aspect of your swing, yes. But not on the golf course.

The only way a swing key can be helpful when you are playing is if you have a positive habit that relates to that key. Just because you think something doesn't mean that your body's going to execute it automatically. The thought has to be grounded in something your body already has learned to do.

If you don't have a habit in place, a swing key is not going to create one on the spot. Ben Hogan used to say that he never played a shot he hadn't practiced a thousand times. Now, a thousand times is a little daunting for mere mortals, but the idea is absolutely sound.

You'll hear a tour player talk about a swing key from time to time, but keep in mind that he's already practiced what he's preaching. And that key many times pertains to his forward swing, rarely his backswing.

SWING AS HARD AS YOU CAN

Arnold Palmer told me that when he was a youngster, his dad used to tell him the same thing that Jack Grout told Jack Nicklaus at a similar age: hit the ball as hard as you can.

That, in my opinion, is perfect advice for kids just taking up golf. Just try to kill it. Go for distance first, then direction. Learn by trial and error the fine line between maximum effort and out of control. Do that, and I guarantee that the young golfer will decide, on his own, that he has to find some way, some technique, some philosophy—though he might not use that term—for keeping the ball in play.

The golf swing doesn't feel natural. It's something you learn, not something you're born with. If you start kids with a whole lot of technical stuff and tell them they have to curb their natural instinct to whack the daylights out of the ball, they'll fight you every step of the way. They're too busy having fun, too busy playing the game, to want to stop and learn a lot of mumbo jumbo.

You let kids hit away. Let them learn to use the club to make the ball go, the way they learn to hit a baseball. Then, when they're ready, when they're pretty good at finding the ball with the club head, you begin to introduce technique, balance, and rhythm bit by bit.

That doesn't work with adults. Their egos are more fragile. They need instant results. They're less willing to learn from their mistakes. They're more worried about how they look in front of other golfers. They're working the game, not playing it. And, compared with kids, most adults are slow learners.

Plus they're not as good at finding their ball in the rough when they do hit it crooked.

ATTENTION, SUCCESSFUL BUSINESSMEN: REMEMBER WHAT GOT YOU WHERE YOU ARE

Sometimes I think that notice should be prominently displayed in clubhouses, on golf carts, perhaps even stamped on golf balls.

As a rule, successful business executives are very difficult to teach. They're accustomed to success. They're impatient with failure. They're accustomed to solving problems quickly and definitively by using their minds.

But in golf, you solve problems with your body, impatience is ruinous, and failure is frequent—it has to be, if you define success as par.

Businessmen who are successful in their fields want and expect to be just as successful at golf. Fair enough. But it's hard for them to accept that golf can be as difficult as it is and that it can take as much time as it does to acquire proficiency. After all, it's only a game.

Successful people need to remember what made them successful in the first place. When a businessman complains to me that his golf game is not improving, I'll ask him, "If you only went into the office once a week for about five hours, would you be as successful as you are?"

WHAT ARE YOU DOING FOR THE NEXT SIX MONTHS?

A major swing change takes time. If you've sliced the ball all your golfing life, you're not going to learn to draw it overnight. Sounds reasonable, right? But there's always somebody who doesn't achieve instant success and then comes to one of two conclusions—either "Flick didn't give me the right information" or "I can't do it."

I tell anyone who seems committed to making a major change, "You've probably got six months of hard work to do to fix the problem." When I say that, I can almost hear the student's mental calculator short-circuit: "Holy Toledo, this guy Flick's talking about six months to change one bad habit, and I've got ten bad habits. That's *five* years."

My answer: "If we can solve your number one problem, it will help the others get better."

The good news is that even though there may be ten problems, most of the time they're related to posture or aim or grip or some other pre-swing error—usually a combination—which you can correct without even going to the golf course. Do you have a mirror in your bedroom? Then you can practice correct setup posture every day before your morning coffee.

The reason I give people time parameters is because so many folks are looking for a quick fix. They've spent a lifetime perfecting a bad swing, but they want to learn a good one by next weekend.

Sorry, but it can't be done.

○ ○ ○

The Golfer's Oath

I, [*state your own name enthusiastically*], do solemnly swear to the Golf Gods that I shall be my own best friend while on the Training Ground and on the Playing Ground. So help me, Golf Gods.

THE VALUE OF INSTANT REPLAY

Sam Snead and I were having lunch one day at Pine Tree in Boynton Beach, Florida. It was back in the mid-eighties, and I was working on an instructional article with Sam. A man walked up to our table with a copy of a book that Sam had written back before World War II and asked him to sign it. Sam said sure, he'd be happy to, and asked the man where he'd like him to sign it. The man opened the book to a picture and said right here, right on this picture of you.

"That was a seven iron at the PGA Championship in Hershey, Pennsylvania," Sam said as he was signing, "and I drew the ball." Then he pointed to another picture on the opposite page, and he said, "That was a four iron at the U.S. Open at Oakmont, and that ball faded."

And Sam proceeded to flip through the book, stopping at each picture and telling a little story about each shot that was shown. I mean, it was forty-five years later, and Sam was not only able to remember the place and the situation and the club but the ball flight.

Almost all great athletes seem to have an uncanny ability to recall performances in minute detail. Ask Greg Maddux about a game he pitched five years ago, and I'll bet you he can tell you how he worked every batter, what he threw on what count, and what the batter did. (He can probably do the same for a round of golf. Along with John Smoltz and Tom Glavine in that great Atlanta rotation, Maddux is a good golfer.)

And it's not just athletes. The retention qualities of most successful people in whatever field border on the incredible. They remember things they did years and years ago because they need those experiences to continue to develop and grow. I'm not talking about some photographic memory thing. I'm talking about retention that's grounded in a powerful desire to improve. I'm talking about retention as a tool.

Now, sometimes I ask a guy coming off the golf course, "How'd you play today?" And he'll say, "Oh, not very good." So I'll ask, "How'd you play thirteen?" And he'll scratch his head and go, "Let's see now, thirteen . . . is thirteen the long par three?"

Hell, he's only been playing there twenty years, and he still can't remember which hole thirteen is. Obviously the game of golf is not too high on his priority list. How in the world is he going to develop the mind-set to improve his game?

(If I sound like an old scold here, then maybe I am a little, and I apologize. But I never want to leave the impression that there is some easy, no-effort, click-your-heels-and-you're-in-Kansas way to a better golf game. Can you maximize your natural ability without the right mind-set and commitment? No. Can you still enjoy the game of golf? Absolutely. And that's okay: you make your choice based on what your lifestyle permits. But I assume that you want to get *better* or you wouldn't be reading this book.)

After every round, make it a habit to replay it, shot by shot, in your mind. Try to form a precise mental picture of every good shot you made. Don't do that with the bad ones, however. Selective memory is necessary in golf: acknowledge your bad shots, just as you did on your scorecard, then put them out of your memory and move on. The idea behind this exercise is to develop your ability to retain images and experiences that will give you *positive* reinforcement the next time you're on the golf course.

Let other people count sheep. As you're drifting off to sleep, play back the good shots you made earlier in the day. I can't absolutely guarantee that it will knock down your handicap, but I promise you it will make for sweeter dreams.

IT'S NOT BRAIN SURGERY . . . THANK GOODNESS

I'll get a doctor sometimes who won't be making much progress with his game, and he'll be very frustrated and getting angry with himself, so I'll say, "Help me remember, Doctor; how long did it take you to go through med school? Three years?" And then I'll say, "Well, I know golf may not be as hard as medicine, but it took you twelve years to get through elementary school and high school, another four years in college, and then three years in med school. Now, once you got out of med school, were you ready to do all the procedures you can do now? No? That's right, you did your internship and your couple of years of residency. And now you can *practice* medicine."

By now, he's getting my point, namely, that you're not going to become proficient at the game of golf, mentally or physically, without an investment of time and energy.

Most of the people I see tell me they're looking for dramatic improvement in their games. That doctor, for instance, will tell me, "I want to get really good at this." And I say, "Okay. How much time can you play?" "Oh, I can play on the weekends." I say, "Okay. I'm going to let you go into your office and practice operating one day a week. How good would you be on the operating table if you did it one day a week?"

The Golf Gods aren't going to let you get good at the game if you don't have the time to work at it. But they will let you have a good time playing it, provided you have realistic expectations. The wonderful thing about golf, as opposed to brain surgery, is that you don't have to be good at it to enjoy it, *provided you have realistic expectations.* In golf, the first step toward getting better is accepting that you will never be perfect.

BE PREPARED

The hardest thing in golf is to keep yourself in a positive frame of mind so that you don't defeat yourself.

I'm not sure anyone has it instinctively. When you make a bad shot, especially if it results from mental sloppiness or neglect of something fundamental, the natural thing is to want to beat yourself up. You have to train yourself *not* to do the natural thing. You have to train yourself to accept what happens and prepare to go on.

Believe me, I know this from firsthand experience. When I was playing competitive golf, in college and afterward, I thought every shot had to be perfect. When I hit a bad one, I would get all bent out of shape and start lacerating myself for being a dumb, no-talent, worthless . . . well, you can fill in the rest. Especially if you've been there yourself.

Let me tell you a story that illustrates a better approach to the game.

One time about twenty years ago Davis Love, Jr., and I were partners in a match. I'd been scraping it around all day, getting madder and madder at myself, but Davis had been solid and we came into eighteen with a chance to win. But I hooked my tee shot over behind a tree, leaving myself with no shot to the green. That meant it was all up to Davis. And so naturally I got hot and started cursing myself. "Partner," I said to Davis, "I'm really sorry to be such a heavy load today."

Well, Davis looked at me, and he smiled, and he said, "You don't understand. This is what I have lived and practiced for in golf, to have a chance to enjoy this kind of challenge."

Davis used to say, "Prepare for success, accept what happens, then get ready for your next shot." I don't think I've ever heard a better, more succinct statement about the attitude we should all bring to the game of golf.

If you think about it, it works pretty well for life, too.

> **"Prepare for success, accept what happens, then get ready for your next shot."**
>
> —Davis Love, Jr.

WHISTLE WHILE YOU WORK

Everybody who's watched him on TV knows that Fuzzy Zoeller whistles while he's walking down the fairway. He looks so natural and carefree. You see somebody whistling, it's pretty easy to conclude that he's not concentrating all that hard on the business at hand, that he has a happy-go-lucky, I-don't-care attitude. And it's not a big jump to conclude that a guy like that can't be much of a competitor. Good old easygoing Fuzzy.

Well, let me tell you, "good old easygoing Fuzzy" is one of the grittiest competitors in golf. If he hadn't had such serious and chronic trouble with his back over the years, there's no telling how many more tournaments he would have won. When a match is on the line, he's about as easygoing as a wolverine.

The fact is, Fuzzy's whistling is a habit that he formed *quite consciously* to help keep his emotions on an even keel so that he can play the next shot rather than replay the last one.

Think about it: if you're whistling, it's pretty hard to yell at yourself.

NONATHLETES WELCOME

Occasionally you'll hear someone say that you don't need good athletic skills to be a good golfer. My response is "Oh, so when did eye-hand coordination, timing, determination, and the ability to perform under pressure stop being athletic skills?"

What *is* true is that not all the traditional athletic skills are required to play golf. For instance, I would put Arnold Palmer in the ninety-ninth percentile as a static athletic performer. He's one of the best pool players I've ever seen; I think he won the pool championship on tour a couple of times. But when he's in motion, when he's shooting a basketball or catching a football, Arnold is a very average athlete. On the flip side of that, Julius Erving was one of the most physically graceful, athletically gifted players ever to touch a basketball. But with a golf club in his hands, Dr. J is only slightly better than average, even though he loves the game, studies it, and plays a lot.

Then you have a rare individual like Danny Ainge, who seems to be able to do everything. He played major-league baseball. He had a long career in the NBA. When he was at Brigham Young University, he used to work out with Steve Young, and I understand that Young thought Ainge had terrific promise as a wide receiver and tried to persuade him to play football. He's an accomplished skier. And he's a fine golfer—he plays to a four handicap.

So where does a Tom Kite fit into this equation? Tom, by his own admission, is not near the athlete that, say, Ben Crenshaw is. But Tom made himself into a great golfer through will, determination, and one of the most extraordinary work ethics the world has ever seen.

The point is that I'm not about to allow a student to tell me, "Oh, I can't play golf, I'm not athletic enough" any more than I'm going to pay much attention to someone who says, "I'm a real good athlete, so golf is going to be easy."

Athleticism is a desirable trait for a golfer, but nothing is as important as attitude.

The best reason I can think of for playing the ball down—not playing winter rules, not rolling it once in the fairway, not flipping the ball out of a divot—is not just because that's what the Rules of Golf tell you to do. Playing it down helps you learn to adjust to different conditions, to deal with reality, to recover from bad breaks, and to test yourself honestly.

HAVE A DREAM

I don't like the term "self-hypnosis." There's too much mystique associated with the word "hypnosis," and there's an implication that not everybody can do it. I also don't think the term "visualization" goes far enough. I prefer to talk about having a dream.

When you create a dream about a ball following a trajectory to a target, or a putt rolling into the back of the cup, or a ball coming softly out of the sand, you put your body at ease. When you reach this positive dream state, you get more relaxed. You feel warmer. You see yourself making the swing effortlessly, smoothly.

Athletes will sometimes talk about a "moment in space" where they are playing well and everything is moving in slow motion, or maybe not at all. Race car drivers say that when they're driving well, they're not even aware of the speed they're moving at because they're so in control of themselves and their machine that they can move in and out of traffic without feeling as if it has to be done abruptly. Divers talk about standing on the end of the platform and seeing themselves making the dive before they take off. Hitters in baseball talk about "seeing the ball," and basketball players talk about being "in a zone."

Ask a tour player who's in a streak in which he never sees the wrong side of seventy what it feels like, and chances are he'll tell you there's no sense of effort or swinging at all, there's never a moment's hesitation about what club to use. It's almost a trancelike state.

Sometimes the dream just happens—you find yourself in it, however briefly, and suddenly you find yourself playing to your very peak, if only for a few holes or even a few swings.

But I believe you can train yourself to invoke a dream and use it in preparing to make a shot.

Fuzzy Zoeller says that anytime he has an approach shot that is especially significant, he replays in his mind a shot he made in 1979 during the play-off to win his Masters. It was an eight iron that he hit stiff at the eleventh green to set up a birdie to beat Tom Watson and Ed Snead. Fuzzy remembers how effortless it felt, how easy it was. He calls on that dream to help him when he's facing a particularly difficult shot.

Now, anybody who plays golf fairly regularly—even a player who has never seen the sunny side of one hundred—has hit some good shots. Not as many as Fuzzy, granted, but enough to draw on to create a dream or two that can be used during a Pre-Shot Routine. What you're doing is training yourself to think about good shots, not bad ones, as you prepare to make your next Shot. This calms and relaxes your muscles so you can perform at your best.

You may surprise yourself at how many times your dream will come true.

GET REAL

Not long ago I asked Jack Nicklaus to tell me, based on his experience in pro-ams over the years, what he felt was the most important flaw in the golf games of amateurs.

As a golf teacher, I expected him to identify one of the common flaws I routinely see: bad alignment and aim, bad grip, bad posture. Most golf instructors, I suspect, would also point to something physical or technical. So I was surprised, at first, by Jack's reply.

"Most amateurs have an unrealistic evaluation of their talent level, and as a consequence they attempt to play shots that they can't execute," Jack said. "A twenty tries to play like a ten, and an eight tries to hit shots that would be tough for a scratch player."

A little puzzled at first, I then realized that Jack was responding as a *player.* Consequently, he didn't mention anything physical or technical. He focused on scoring, which is, after all, what the game is all about.

The logic of what he was saying is that a twenty handicapper might, with a *realistic* evaluation of his talent level, steer clear of high-risk shots beyond his capabilities—and, in the process, maybe bring his handicap down to a seventeen.

If you are going to be your own coach—and I want you to be—then you need to be frank and objective in your evaluation of your talent—the way any coach has to be.

"THE LONGER IT TAKES ME TO GET IT, THE LONGER I WILL KEEP IT"

The learning process is very fragile—the last thing you learn will probably be the first thing you lose because that habit has not been ingrained long enough. That's why focused repetition is so important and why better golfers are constantly returning to the basics.

Susie Maxwell Berning was one of the first players of national standing with whom I worked back when I was the head professional at the Losantiville Country Club in Cincinnati. She first came to me for help with her alignment and setup, and from there we moved on to her swing and her overall game.

Susie was a wonderfully talented athlete, but she wasn't about to settle for what she could accomplish on talent alone. That is precisely the attitude that I associate with successful people—a work ethic that's rooted in the understanding of the relationship between effort and achievement. And it was that work ethic, along with her talent, that was the key to Susie's three U.S. Open titles.

One time, after finishing second or third in a tournament in St. Louis, she drove directly to Cincinnati—a pretty long haul at the end of a workday, but we had a lesson scheduled for eight-thirty Monday morning and Susie wasn't about to miss it.

Well, it was a typical July day in Cincinnati: hot and humid—especially humid. She was working on a swing change, so she must have hit balls for two and a half, three hours, and she hadn't hit three good shots. Finally, I said to her, "Susie, I know it's really disappointing having played so well this past weekend, to be working this hard and not to be able to find your golf ball."

"No big deal, Jim," she said. "The longer it takes me to get it, the longer I'll keep it."

BIG PICTURE

Jack Nicklaus has often said that if he works on anything, it goes through his whole golf swing. In other words, if he's trying to do something with his full swing, he wants to do it with his chipping and pitching as well. Many good players feel that whatever they're working on relates to their whole game. They might work on one thing, but they have the whole picture in mind because that one element is found in all parts of the game.

When I first started working with Tom Lehman, he used to hate to practice bunker shots because the outside-in path of the forward swing he used in the sand was directly contrary to the inside path he favored on his full-swing shots. I remember that we spent about six hours one Saturday making an adjustment to turn his bunker swing into what is essentially a shorter version of his full swing, that is, with a slight inside-along-the-target-line to inside swing path on the forward swing. This helps him feel that all parts of his golf game are part of a single whole.

With people who are in the early stages of developing their golf swing, I like working around the green on chipping and pitching because there it's easier to sense what the club is doing and feel its contact with the golf ball. In fact, I believe this so strongly I'd like to see the following plea implanted in your memory—or at the very least embroidered on your golf towel:

If you're having trouble with your full swing, go back and work on your part shot. If you're having trouble with that, go back and work on your putting. Let your short game be a guide back to the full swing.

TRAIN YOUR SELECTIVE MEMORY

Ask a professional golfer about bad shots he's hit and chances are he'll refuse to talk about them—and for a very good reason. A mental image of a good swing will help you repeat; so will a mental image of a bad swing.

The average golfer hits more bad shots than good ones—true. But he's hit enough good ones to call to mind those situations, which help him hit better shots. In assessing a round

ARMADILLO WILLY'S #10
3 – SAN MATEO

Check	Table	Cov	Server	Time	Date
151636	C&C	1	12	4:19:49 PM	7/5/01

1	ZBURGER	5.29
1	SM FRIES	1.99
	Food Sub-Total	7.28
	SUB TOTAL	7.28
	Sales Tax	0.58
	TOTAL	**7.86**
	Visa	7.86
		======
	Change	0.00
	Amount due	0.00

THANK YOU,
BILLY

BOTTOM OF PAGER
HAS YOUR NUMBER!

ARMADILLO WILLY'S #10
3 SAN MATEO
Check Table Cov Server Time Date
10196 L&C-F 12 4 1:18:49 PM 7/6/01

1 [illegible]	5.29
1 [illegible]	1.99
Food Sub Total	7.28
SUB TOTAL	7.28
Sales Tax	0.58
TOTAL	7.86
Visa	7.86
Change	0.00
Amount due	0.00

THANK YOU
BILLY

BOTTOM OF PAGER
HAS YOUR NUMBER!

you've just played, you naturally will have to deal with the shots that didn't come off. But instead of obsessing on what you did wrong, focus on what you need to do right the next time.

Every golfer needs to keep memories of good shots at the front of his consciousness and immediately accessible. The bad memories? Lock them up and throw away the key.

THE WINNER AND STILL CHAMPION . . .

Imagine knowing that you are going to win every golf tournament you play in. Not thinking you're going to win, or believing it, but *knowing* it.

Lyle Anderson is a gentleman who has developed a number of great golf-residential communities, including Desert Highlands and Desert Mountain in Scottsdale and Las Campañas in Santa Fe. He is one of the most creative people in golf today, and he just flat-out loves to play. What's interesting is that he *knows*—knows before he even tees off—that he is going to win the championship in every pro-am, every club tournament, every match of any kind he plays.

The *attitude* championship.

Lyle looks at it this way: he can't always control where his ball goes, and he can't control the bad bounces and unlucky breaks—but he can control his attitude. And he says he *will* win the attitude championship every time he tees it up.

He makes the people he's playing with have fun. He's not a bitcher and complainer. He's not a crybaby when he's got a bad streak going. He's not going to let his own frustrations about his game slop over and distract his playing partners. And he's not going to lose sight of the fact that the only reason for a nonprofessional to play golf is to have fun.

Don't you think that's spectacular?

SCORECARD SUMMARY

- Golf is like life: to gain success, you must be able to learn from failure.
- Replacing bad habits with good ones means going through a period of being uncomfortable.
- Be frank and objective in your evaluation of your talent.
- Key Concept: *The attitude you bring to the game of golf will ultimately determine the level of proficiency you attain in it.*

EPILOGUE

LATE IN THE FALL of 1995, well after the Ryder Cup, Tom Lehman and I met at Desert Mountain in Scottsdale for a work session. As we always do at the end of a golf season, we reviewed what Tom had accomplished in 1995 and talked about his goals for 1996. It was then that I told him that I thought he had it in him to become the best player in the world.

Why would you say that? he asked.

Because you possess something that I can't teach, I told him. You have a special gift for making your swing repeat, time and time and time again. You have your life in balance, as well as your golf game. You have the self-confidence and the self-knowledge to be your own coach.

Perhaps I planted the seed, but Tom made the commitment—not just to be good, not just to get better, but to become the best player in the world.

And he did.

Tom Lehman's accomplishments in 1996 capped six years of hard work. He had it in him. I just helped him find it. And while I may be prejudiced, I think he'll keep it for a long, long time.

The program that Tom has followed since we began working together is based on a simple but bedrock concept, namely, that it is the use of the club head to put the ball in the target area that creates motion and rhythm in the golf swing.

Not mechanics.

Not positions.

The use of the club head.

It is a concept that I first learned from Bob Toski and that I have later had reinforced by working with Jack Nicklaus.

Both the Professional Swing and the Developmental Swing, as I have explained them in this book, are rooted in that basic premise: it is the use of the golf club to put the ball in the target area that creates motion and rhythm in the golf swing.

The swinging of the golf club turns the body.

The body turns in response to the swinging of the golf club.

Not vice versa.

That concept works for the best player ever to play the game. It works for the 1996 Player of the Year. And I believe it can work for you.

ACKNOWLEDGMENTS

NO ONE MAKES it through a life as rich and rewarding as mine has been without the help, inspiration, and guiding example of many people along the way. My only regret is that I would need another book to express my gratitude adequately. And my only fear is that I might inadvertently leave someone off the list that follows. It's enough to give a fellow the yips.

Good players don't make good teachers, and vice versa—right? Dead wrong, at least if the teacher-player in question happens to bear the name Bob Toski. The leading money winner on the PGA Tour in 1954 when he had four victories, Bob became a consummate teacher. No teacher in my experience has ever demonstrated a greater sensitivity for the golf swing and a better feel for playing the game. His unstinting generosity in sharing his knowledge and understanding has made my career fun.

Since the beginning of this decade, I have been privileged to work for the greatest player in the history of golf—and I never cease to be amazed by Jack Nicklaus's insights into every aspect of the game. My goal, as a teacher, is to nurture and communicate his principles and his philosophy through the Nicklaus-Flick Golf School. I consider this a sacred trust.

Speaking of trust, I owe a special debt of gratitude to Tom Lehman for his trust in me these past several years. Nothing in my professional life has pleased me more than helping Tom find his game. His courage, determination, and integrity have been nothing short of inspirational. He is a true champion.

Arnold Palmer and I roomed together for a brief period at Wake Forest, and we were teammates on the Deacons golf team, which makes me one of the first to experience, up close and personal, his unquenchable competitive fire. Know what? I could tell back then he was going to be a pretty fair golfer.

Way back in 1955, at the Evansville Country Club in Evansville, Indiana, Don Fischesser gave me the chance to take my first step in what became a life journey. Without his support, I might still be pumping gas back in Bedford.

A creative entrepreneur with amazing people skills, Bill Laughlin has been a constant source of wise counsel, moral support, and genuine friendship for fifteen years—and counting.

Over the years I've written hundreds of thousands of words about how to play the game in various books and magazines, many of which would have been unplayable lies without the guidance, support, and friendship of a small army of editors and writers. Among those who helped turn my ideas into printable English: Dick Aultman, John Andrisani, Ken Bowden, Larry Dennis, Jim Frank, and Roger Schiffman.

The most important "golf muscle" is the one between your ears. No people understand that better than Maynard Howe, Bob Rotella, and Dick Coop, three brilliant sports psychologists who know that the key to straightening out your slice often begins with straightening out your head. Each has helped me mightily in my continuing exploration of the links between the mental and the physical aspects of the game.

They say you're judged by the company you keep. I certainly hope so, because no one could ever ask for a finer bunch of colleagues than the teachers I've worked with, argued with, and learned with in a lifetime in golf. Among them, in alphabetical order, are Chuck Cook, Gardner Dickinson, John Elliott, Charlie Epps, Jack Grout, Martin Hall, John Jacobs, Gary Knapp, Peter Kostis, Davis Love, Jr., Jack Lumpkin, Bill MacWilliam, Mike Malaska, Willie Ogg, Harvey Penick, Dean Reinmuth, Paul Runyan, Irv Schloss, Laird Small, Bill Strausbaugh, Stan Thirsk, Gary Wiren, and Mark Wood.

Upwards of 25 million men and women in America play golf. Way less than a thousand play it well enough to survive on the various professional tours. But even more than their amazing talent, the thing I respect most about the tour players—both men and women—is their courage. With no guaranteed long-term contracts, no disabled lists when they suffer injuries, and no teammates to pick them up when they go into a slump, they are truly a breed apart among today's athletes. Talk about an elite group!

It's been my good fortune to learn so much from many of those Fairway Warriors—in some cases as a coach, in others only in conversation about an aspect of the game, sometimes as a friend. Among them: Tommy Aaron, John Adams, Paul Azinger, Butch Baird, Miller Barber, Frank Beard, Susie Maxwell Berning, Ronnie Black, Phil Blackmar, Jane Blaylock, Mark Brooks, George Burns, Fred Couples, Bruce Crampton, Elaine Crosby, Brad Faxon, Jim Ferree, Fred Funk, Tim Herron, Scott Hoch, Ed Humenik, Caroline Keggi, Tom Kite, Bernhard Langer, Gene Littler, Lyn Lott, Andrew Magee, Phil Mickelson, Cary Middlecoff, Cathy Morse, Larry Mowry, Byron Nelson, Jack O'Keefe, DeDe Owens, Gary Player, Tom Purtzer, Judy Rankin, Loren Roberts, Chi Chi Rodriguez, Gordon Sherry, Tom Sieckmann, Vijay Singh, J. C. Snead, Sam Snead, Hollis Stacy, Lanny Wadkins, Tom Watson, Tom Weiskopf, Ian Woosnam, and the late Bert Yancey.

It's always been a special delight to observe how superior athletes in other sports respond to the challenges of golf. I've had a chance to help the likes of Charles Barkley, Ralph Beard, Hubie Brown, Seth Joyner, Jim Kaat, Whitey Ford, Stan Mikita, and Bobby Rahal fine-tune their "second loves." They've taught me a lot about the heart of an athlete. So, for that matter, has a non-athlete who nonetheless possesses outstanding athletic skills: the great dancer (and improving golfer), Mikhail Baryshnikov.

Teachers learn as much (if not more) from their students as vice versa. I'll forever be grateful for what I've learned from great students like Lyle Anderson, Anne Archer, Roone Arledge, Larry Bianchi, Bob Brink, Ely Callaway, Tom Crowe, Jim Davis, Len Decof, Joe Dionne, Ted Forstmann, Ed Haber, Dr. Jay Hall, Rick Karas, Ken Kendrick, Peter Kessler, Everett Kircher, Joe Lee, Gene Lilley, Charles Mechem, Jim Montgomery, Bob Oelman, Bob Reynolds, Milt Schloss, Phil Schneider, Ralph Schulz, Greg Shanik, Barry Smith, Hal Sperlich, John Stuart, Lou Susman, and Dan Tully.

Illustrations for some of the ideas in these pages came from the talented pen of Mona Mark, whose skill is exceeded only by her patience. At Villard Books, Amy Scheibe kept her cool while keeping the project on track. Copy editor Jeff Smith proved once again that a good eraser is the golfer's best friend.

Finally, three people deserve primary credit for helping put this book in your hands. Len Riggio, a man of amazing imagination and vision, saw something in my teaching philosophy that he liked. Peter Gethers, an editor of surpassing creativity and passion, set up the match. And Glen Waggoner, a writer whose good humor and loyal support never flagged, deftly guided my club selection. If the result isn't bogey-free, it surely isn't their fault. I'd be pleased to form a foursome with this trio anytime.

ABOUT THE AUTHORS

A native of Bedford, Indiana, JIM FLICK graduated from Wake Forest University in 1952. Except for a tour of military service during the Korean War, he has been teaching golf ever since—first at two golf clubs in Indiana, then at the Losantiville Country Club in Cincinnati. He was a senior instructor for the *Golf Digest* schools and is (since 1991) director of education and training of the Nicklaus-Flick Golf School, of which he is the co-founder. He has been Jack Nicklaus's personal coach since 1990.

Over the years, Flick has worked with over two hundred other touring professionals, including two three-time U. S. Women's Open champions, Hollis Stacy and Susie Maxwell Berning, and Tom Lehman, 1996 British Open Champion and PGA Tour Player of the Year. But he has also taught many thousands of amateurs, ranging from junior golfers to beginners to advanced players.

Honored by the PGA of America as their 1988 Teacher of the Year, Flick has hosted more golf schools than any teacher in the profession and has lectured at numerous PGA seminars and workshops. He has written instructional books, articles, and videos. In 1996 he was the keynote speaker at the PGA Summit, a biannual congregation of teaching professionals.

Flick and his wife, Geri, currently reside in Scottsdale, Arizona, where he is director of instruction at Desert Mountain.

A Texan by birth and a New Yorker by choice, GLEN WAGGONER is the author of two books about golf, *Divots, Shanks, Gimmes, Mulligans, and Chili Dips: A Life in 18 Holes* and *The Traveling Golfer*. He is also a co-author of two other books, *Baseball by the Rules* and *Esquire Etiquette*. In addition, he is one of the founders of Rotisserie League Baseball and has edited all eleven editions of *Rotisserie League Baseball: The Official Rule Book and Draft-Day Guide*. He has written extensively about golf and other sports, cooking, health

OUT THE AUTHORS

el, people, manners, even fashion, for various na- nes, including *Golf, Senior Golfer, Esquire,* and *Men's* ere he is a contributing editor and featured columnist. es and essays have also appeared in *The New York Times,* *ago Tribune, Baseball Weekly,* and *USA Today*. He is also ed- *ESPN Magazine,* an all-sports biweekly.